Jane

TO BEACH OR NOT TO BEACH?

With Best Wishes

Mary

29th June 2024

For my Family, sister-in-law Marie, niece Emily and husband
Steven, nephews Peter and Michael, their wives Jennie and
Catherine and youngsters Lucas, Harriet, Eliza, Arthur
and Daphne along with memories of my brother John,
who sadly died while the book was being written.
Love you all – 'Old Aunt'

Front cover – main image

M.E.W. visiting the ladies of the Warao tribe (the boat people) at their stilt house above the Orinoco River, Venezuela, 1993. These good people use bongos, homemade wooden canoes, for transportation as walking is difficult amongst the hundreds of streams, marshes and high waters of their great river. Warao babies and toddlers are known for their ability to hold on tight and often learn to both paddle and swim before they can walk (I noticed that their legs were very short. Is this the evolution of generations of not walking much? I was on my knee for this photograph to be taken).

Rear cover – main image

Antarctica.

TO BEACH OR NOT TO BEACH?

Tongue-in-cheek memories of some of Mary's challenges, catastrophes, lessons, experiences and thorough enjoyment from a lifetime of travels

MARY E. WHEILDON

BREWIN BOOKS

BREWIN BOOKS
19 Enfield Ind. Estate,
Redditch,
Worcestershire,
B97 6BY
www.brewinbooks.com

Published by Brewin Books 2024

A CIP catalogue record for this book is available from the British Library.

ISBN: 978-1-85858-773-8

Printed and bound in Great Britain
by Hobbs The Printers Ltd.

Contents

Acknowledgements

My thanks go firstly, to Gill Ashley Smith, who has patiently and most diligently kept me on the straight and narrow through the writing of this book. Living next door, we were able to pass the memory stick over the garden fence during the Covid lock downs, since then editing has been far more social and great fun especially with my unconventional way of writing! My thanks too, to my dear friend Bob Ellis for his generous introduction and to Alistair Brewin my Publisher. Without the tremendous help given by Adrian of Trailfinders and Justin of DialAFlight, many of these trips would never have happened.

Enormous thanks to all those dear friends and relatives who have either invited me to travel with them or have accepted the suggestion that they might come with me on an expedition into the unknown, and to those who I have met along the way who have amazingly joined me, in search of once again, waiting to have their 'breath taken away'!

Thanks to all those of you who have enjoyed the tremendous sights, sounds and wonderful scents; suffered dire heat, dreadful aromas and delays with me; helped get us out of a predicament, extricate ourselves from yet another situation and thankfully kept your sense of humour whatever the catastrophe. We have had some terrific fun, survived, come home with fantastic tales and all too soon found ourselves hankering for the next adventure.

I trust that this fun read will bring back memories; I appreciate I will have missed out so much but hopefully this will spark happy thoughts of travels enjoyed together.

Introduction

I first met Mary Wheildon more than 50 years ago at The Warwick Boat Club where we played sport. During these 5 decades I have grown to value Mary's friendship highly and developed a great respect for her amazing energy and burning desire to visit all corners of the world in search of rich experiences. I am sure you will be intrigued as you read her captivating and hilarious account of her life travelling worldwide.

Mary is a first-class organiser and well known for arranging superb holidays and in galvanizing help for many different events and activities, including charity work. She has tireless energy, she is a first-class cook, hardworking and has terrific enthusiasm. She is great company on a voyage with a keen sense of humour, so vital as you travel far and wide.

I have been lucky to share a handful of holidays with Mary, mainly wildlife centred excursions to observe birds, flowers and other fauna and flora. You can guarantee you will have an action-packed holiday with rich experiences because of her detailed research of destinations and list of sights you cannot miss. What is amazing is that she is not put off organizing trips following crises and dangerous episodes when most people would take years to get over these problems. For example, on a most memorable voyage with Mary to St Kilda, cruising way out off the Outer Hebrides, we encountered stormy seas and poor Mary was dreadfully seasick and spent hours lying on the dining room bench. But then she organises a similar holiday the next year where there is a high chance of sea sickness! Take skiing, a passion of hers. On three occasions Mary has been stretchered off the pistes with severe damage to her knee following catastrophic crashes. And yet, a few months later she books another skiing holiday! Not many people would do that. What amazing determination.

Mary has always a new destination in mind and we all look forward to hearing about her exciting escapades. We are so pleased she keeps a diary and is a keen photographer and has described as well as illustrating her experiences in this splendid book.

Dr Bob Ellis

Chapter 1
'To Beach or not to Beach?'

M.E.W. ... not known for beach holidays! ... For so many years my friends have not been in the slightest surprised with my answer to their questions as to where I was off to next. Many have been so kind explaining that there is a war over there, or a disease, plague, flood, drought, hot or too cold and asked why on earth I should ever want to go to that destination. However, they would also want to know all about my experiences afterwards well-knowing that they didn't expect me to be going on a traditional 'bucket-and-spade' beach holiday.

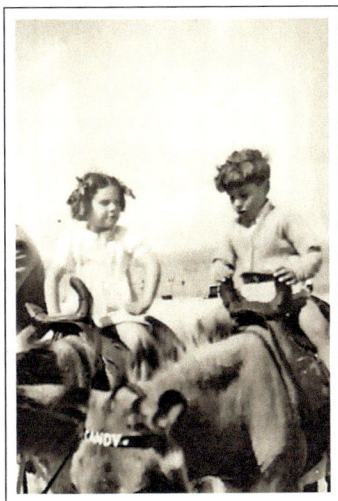

But beaches I have most certainly been on. On my first beach holiday, aged five, we went to Sandown, Isle of Wight with bucket and spade, donkey rides and Punch and Judy shows. My Godmother retired to Southbourne so during the harvest when my parents were so busy I would go down to stay with her for a week or two. I loved it as the water was such fun and I enjoyed visiting the beach huts owned by her friends.

At the age of 21, I was invited by a friend to take a job in Virginia Beach, USA as assistant manageress of the numerous restaurants and room service within The Mariner Hotel, which was right on the ocean front's vast sandy beach. Any free time was spent either surfing, swimming, sunbathing, playing beach volleyball or catching up on lost sleep! I lived with Miss

1

Eleanor, the manageress and sister of John Smith, the hotel owner. In the 1920s and 1930s John and his pals were the first to organise a formal beach service of lifeguarding and chair, umbrella and float rentals along the Virginia Beach ocean front. These lads were the first surfers in the area with heavy wooden boards, but in time the boards evolved, and it was no surprise that Eleanor's son Pete Smith became the renowned East Coast Surf Champion and a legend. He opened the Smith Holland surf shop in the early 60s and it

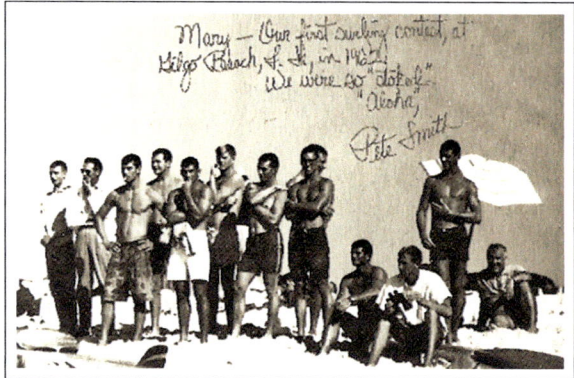

remains a mecca to this day. Surf boards were therefore readily available in our garage and taking a board off the rack one day I was staggered to find an enormous snake curled up asleep at one end. Thankfully I had a surfer friend, a good chum, there to deal with that situation but sadly, even with such a choice of boards I never became an accomplished surfer! During the winter Eleanor and I moved down to the Miramar Hotel, which was her other brother's hotel on Lake Worth, West Palm Beach where I was made Maître d'hôtel working seven days a week from Christmas until Easter. That was terrific fun, hard work, but during my hours off I could cycle to the beach franchise that John had there too beside the famous pier. Sadly, there were never any surfing waves down there that winter, but I was a very lucky girl all the same!

Once back home and running my own business I found myself in an expeditions groove, arriving over the years on some wild, diverse, staggeringly beautiful and most interesting beaches. One evening while up the River Orinoco

2

in Venezuela we went off in our dugouts to a beach for a swim and sunset cocktails. Every one of us was surprised when we landed on a sandbar complete with cool boxes, ideal for our beach! We swam and were joined by freshwater dolphins which were the absolute highlight. Similarly, when sailing on the Great Barrier Reef we were taken to Sudbury Cay for sunset cocktails, again no more than a sandbar.

Arriving in Sri Lanka some years after the awful tsunami that had brought such devastation to the coastal areas, we found some of the coastline had been saved by the mangroves that had not been removed. Sadly, so many across the world have been scrapped in favour of more beach. The provision of safety for the people, let alone a nursery for the young fish, seems to be forgotten by so many in city offices.

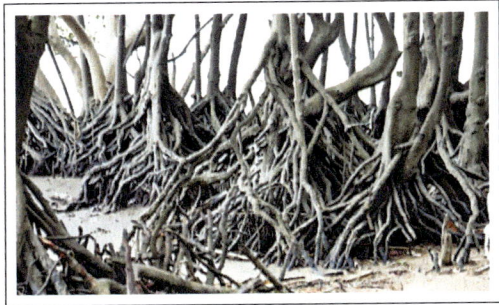

In Durban I was taken on an hour's walk through the black, white and red mangroves, amongst which I could spot the various kinds of crab: red

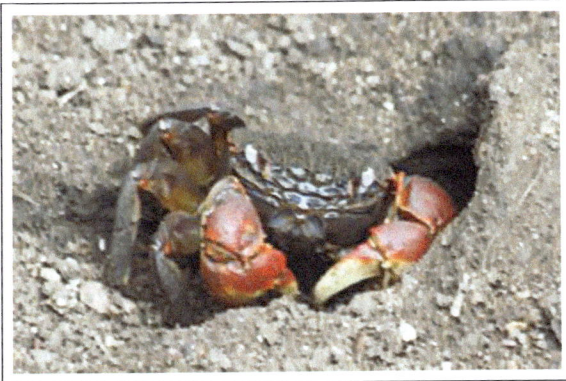

double pincer, fiddler crab and the rare 'tango' crab as well as the mud skippers and climbing whelks, before climbing out onto the dunes and their range of endemic flora. On the east coast of Australia at the Daintree National Park coast we walked through the mangrove boardwalks and onto the beach in search of the crocodiles but, sadly, each time only their tracks were visible! Further south beside the Great Barrier Reef towards Cairns, we sailed up waterways lined with mangroves searching for the last remaining manatees who live there surviving on the lush sea grass – I have since finally sighted one on an early morning walk on Key Biscayne, Florida; apparently it is a regular to that particular spot on the island.

I was most encouraged in Sabah, Borneo where their mangroves, which include five different species, have finally been protected by law. Previously they had been harvested for chipboard predominately for the Japanese market and also for dashboards for the car market before the palm oil market led to even further clearances. Only after the 2005 tsunami was the error realised. We found beautiful beaches too, with the contented friendly residents going about their daily life on and off the water.

While on Liberon Island we sailed over to Turtle Island to visit the turtle project and were immediately thrilled to see the great prints of the turtles who had been up to lay their eggs the previous evening. As night came, we watched as one amazing creature lumbered from the water across the sand to dig a large hole before proceeding to lay 94 eggs. We accompanied the technician as he gathered every one of the turtle eggs into a bucket before the mother turtle finally covered the hole and returned to the ocean. We returned to the nursery where a hole had previously been made to receive the eggs, placed them gently in and covered them with sand to incubate over the next 60 days. The hatchlings that were surfacing that evening were placed into a basket which we were invited to take down to the beach. We gently tipped it on its side and were amazed how quickly the hatchlings tumbled out of the basket to scurry down the beach to the water's edge. To help them go in the right

direction the technician walked backwards shining a torch along the sand, and they followed as if he was the Pied Piper!

After maturity, which is about seven years, the survivors will come back to the same beach to lay eggs every two or three years. I have also walked along beaches at night in search of laying turtles at Kosi Bay, KwaZulu-Natal, S.A., Oman and an incredible coral island off Los Roches which is right at the foot of the Caribbean Islands near Venezuela where the sand was pure ground coral – fabulous.

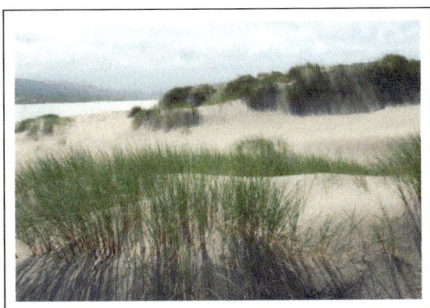

We went ashore on Taransay, Outer Hebrides by zodiac onto the most photogenic beach and sand-spit, the whole area being covered in clumps of machair grass with otter tracks and many flowers. We also landed on East Monach Island where we all wandered off around the sand dunes of the island finding many plants and nesting birds including the infamous fulmars. Two of our professional photographers were determined to make a final attempt at photographing the nesting fulmar, which for its own defence will projectile vomit an unpleasant smelling oleaginous fluid at its aggressors. They succeeded but so did the bird. I stood well back using my long lens!

Given a very wet landing (a big wave filled my wellingtons) by zodiac onto Kayak Island off Prince William Sound, I was allowed three hours to wander along this historic beach. It was the first and only landing site in Alaska in 1741 of Vitus Bering and George Steller, the naturalist. It marks the European discovery of Alaska, where Steller's name is commemorated in many species including the Steller's jay and Steller's sea lion. Captain James Cook also landed there on May

20th, 1778 during his explorations of Alaska. I thoroughly enjoyed the plants, the birds, the geology and the beachcombing. It was pure heaven along that enormous stretch of sand photographing the plants, seaweed, shells and sand markings including tracks of bear and arctic fox. Amongst the birds, I watched a peregrine falcon circling and feeding off a gull's catch, a least-sandpiper and a snipe along with many more common gulls and the most colourful jellyfish I have ever seen. Sadly, Prince William Sound was more recently renowned for the Exxon Valdez disaster.

One July morning we had yet another wet landing on the beach at Woodfjorden, Svalbard. Here the surface was quite rocky underfoot and given a choice of hikes I chose to hike with the flower specialist which was a great success. We clambered up the cliffside looking at all the spring flowers that were working so hard to come out for the so short season. Nothing was more than 5cm high there, even the willow hugged the ground not to be

blown or washed away by the snow melt. We were bombarded by nesting arctic terns, arctic skuas, we also sighted a polar bear slide and wonderful terrain, a most memorable beach indeed. Perhaps even more remarkable was the incredible desert landscape made of pebbles that had been there over millennia when we landed at the beach near Vibebukta. Some of the pebbles had been formed into polygons by the continual snow, ice, permafrost

and thawing. Walking across this terrain was an absolute joy and each step brought yet another amazing sight. Where whale and walrus bones had rested for years plants had rooted appreciating their nutrients, each one of the skeletons providing its own environment. Some of the landscape was just short of modern art, quite abstract. With all this beauty, with the pastel shades and flora, came the saddest sight of all, pollution. The plastic rubbish that lay in a line right along the tidal edge made one want to cry – so far up in the Arctic Circle, miles from any habitation, there was every

type of litter, from coffee jar tops, flipflops, and carrier bags, to picnic cutlery. We gathered enough in a very short time to completely fill a zodiac to take back to our boat, but we hardly touched the surface of that beach, let alone what would land at the next tide.

At the end of August up in the Northwest Passage, the weather was perfect, the water like glass and the temperature 3°C, (which we learned was breaking records). We dressed up in all our wet weather gear for a zodiac trip to the hamlet of Pond Inlet to visit the Inuit village and meet the residents. We landed safely onto a much-used sandy beach and left all our extra clothing spread across various boats and fishing gear that lay there. The villagers came out to welcome us, some in their Inuit dress, and were soon showing us their way of life both along the beach or up in the village.

There are few sandy beaches down on South Georgia, mostly either shale or rocks, over sand, but that mattered not for the sheer beauty and wildlife that we saw down there, almost always with a wet landing!

We were often welcomed by colonies of penguins, seals, elephant seals and numerous other birds along with the local flora or alternatively it was straight from the zodiac into the snow, the beach being a foot or so below – time to work hard, no pain no gain!

I have travelled on most of my Arctic and Antarctic trips with Ice Tracks on whose tours the most wonderful lecturers and guides are provided, keeping

us aware of everything around us and upcoming. On this Antarctic trip we also had a couple of lads who were working for Oceanites, who surveyed the penguin colonies wherever we landed. One morning, we landed by zodiac on Dunno, Michelson Harbour which is a small penguin island right beside majestic hanging glaciers. Landing on the gravelly beach, we walked the snowy hillside sometimes falling into deeper snow, but with poles provided, there wasn't too much of a problem. There were small colonies of Adélie and chinstrap penguins on either side of the island along with a colony of king penguins on the far side with of course the inevitable petrels, brown skuas and sheathbills. It was most amusing watching the penguins cope coming and going from the water, many went about their ablutions in the shore pools, swimming, diving and generally having a very social time all while I listened to their vocalising and the groans and calving of the glacier.

Northeast of Japan we sailed alongside or visited numerous uninhabited islands of the Kuril Islands archipelago. The volcanic calderas and rock formations were spectacular in appearance, and also for their wildlife both in water and on land.

The Yankicha Islands' calderas formed 9,500 years ago in a giant explosion and has had three eruptions in recent centuries. The present fumaroles illustrate that the volcanic history is not yet over. We went off to Yankicha's beautiful caldera which is now flooded by sea water hoping to zodiac inside but sadly the tide was so low that it proved impossible, and nor could we land on

the beach either. Happily, further north we sailed off Matya Island and the islet of Toporkovyy where we were able to zodiac to a pebbly beach heavily covered in many varieties of kelp, plants, waders and more seabirds including common teal, greater scaup, harlequin duck, black scooter and the red faced cormorant.

From the beach we staggered across in our wet weather gear to explore the nature and remains of the Russian air base and radar station. There was a tremendous amount of metal junk strewn amongst the alders, butterburr and other plants I could not identify. Here we enjoyed sightings of shore and land birds as well as visiting the old buildings, the icehouse, toilets, stores and even the old church which was being renovated by some volunteers staying on the island. There were more bunkers and a disused airstrip but throughout my walk there were oil drums, old gas masks and pure bric-a-brac. It was here that I was photographed lying in an old bath on the hillside. Later it formed part of the trip DVD!

We were privileged to be able to land by zodiac on the soft volcanic sand beach on the tiny island of Atlasova, which is part of Kamchatka. Arriving in

the mist we were given three hours to wander to the far point taking in all the plants, which having emerged from the winter's snow, were just beginning to

grow among the many birds and the magnificent scenery. Again, there was a lot of old metalwork, rope, plastic and driftwood lying about as well as many rusty remains of an old herring processing plant. Here there was a good chance of finding the rare Japanese glass floats washed up, so eyes were always on alert –

some of us were successful! The larks were singing, also buntings, ravens, harlequin ducks, pelagic cormorants and even a raptor flew overhead, with dwarf Ragusa roses and small alpine plants just showing their first colours. Even the tracks and holes of the island's rodents and lemmings were

visible. The sand analysed by our geologists was found to be ash layers with embedded volcanic bombs, scoria with basalt pumice also added.

The most remote beach with local human habitation (800) I am ever likely to land upon was on June 5th, 2010. By zodiac we landed at Nikkolskoye Village on Bering Island, one of the Commander Islands located off the

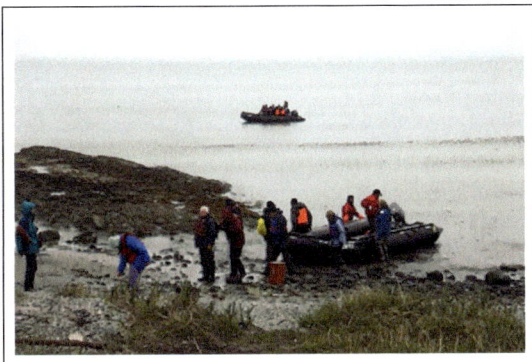

Kamchatka Peninsula in the Bering Sea (55.0'N 166.15.15'E). Roughly 55 miles x 15 miles, it is the largest of the islands, desolate, with severe weather, treeless hills, and mostly foggy and prone to earthquakes. Vitus Bering, sailing in Sviatoi Petr (*St. Peter*), was shipwrecked and died of an illness on this island, along with 28 of his men. The remaining crew survived thanks to the sea otters which were extremely numerous at that time. Vitus was buried with the Lutheran

rites of his home country, Denmark, in this bleak and desolate place. When spring came, the survivors built a new ship out of the remnants of the old one and managed to sail to Kamchatka.

The island is also less commonly known as the 'Floating Island' simply because it floats on the International Date Line! The residents were an absolute delight, so thrilled to receive us as we were their first visiting tourists in three years. It is said that to live there is not much fun, but the locals are really great and don't waste much time complaining about their disastrous realities, instead preferring to tell you one of their countless jokes about themselves! This is just how I found them and for sure there certainly was no bucket, spade and deckchair to be found on their beach!

We also landed that day at Severo-Zapadniy, another

beach on the same island but far more difficult to disembark because of the rough waters. When we finally reached shore, we trundled along the rough beach, onto the tundra, passing a couple of fishermen's huts, up to a hillside to watch the seal rookery below. Another bleak and extraordinarily beautiful landscape.

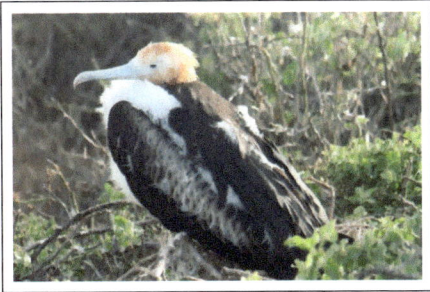

A world away from those bleak beaches was the warm island of Española, in the Galápagos Islands. We travelled a considerable distance by zodiac to the beautiful white sandy beach where we swam and were joined by turtles and seals before I wandered for an hour the length of the beach to enjoy all the flora and fauna. Galápagos sea lions inhabited the beach, hooded mockingbirds, large ground finch, semi-terrestrial hermit crabs, turnstones, turtles offshore and the many indigenous marine iguanas. The plant life included black and button mangrove, Parkinsonia, Palo Santo, bitterbush, spiny bush, velvet bush, Galápagos lantana, beach morning glory and even passionflower. We visited many other fabulous beaches on the various islands that we were booked to visit. The most memorable was at Floreana, where after swimming in the rather cooler waters that morning

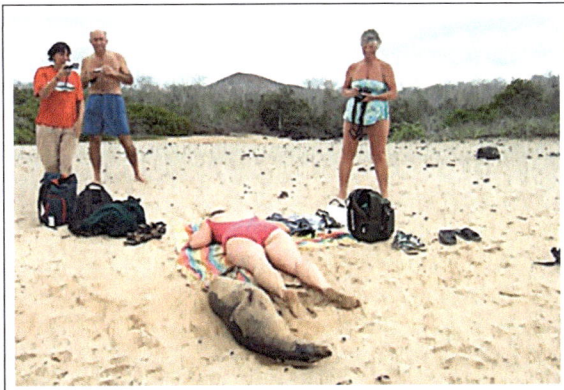

and lying on the beach to dry and warm through, one of our party (whose birthday it happened to be) awoke to find a sea lion had come across and had lain beside her. How cool was that!

I finally put my hands up and admit to the odd grasp at leisure upon a sandy beach, perhaps with a little snorkelling which is what we girls did when visiting Sunshine Beach on Mahé in the Seychelles. Walking there from our self-catering house had been a major

13

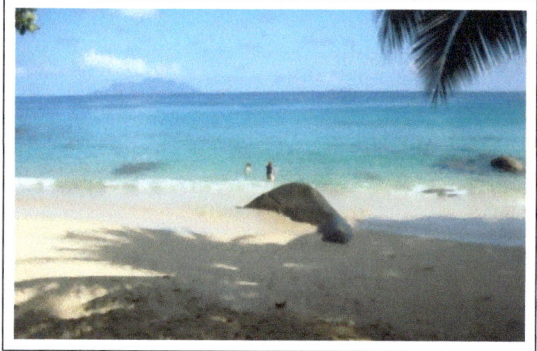

problem as there was the most extensive cobweb, which was home to a huge number of enormous arachnids, right across the road. My friend, with a total phobia to spiders, was frozen to the spot. I must admit I have rarely seen larger spiders but to coax her further down the coast road was difficult. In the end a large black towel was placed over her head and away we went – we returned by bus!

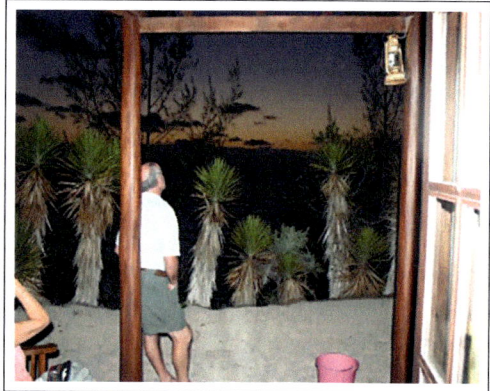

Pure luxury in the middle of a month in Madagascar and for the very first time on any of my expeditions a *day off* was included. We had arrived at the Paradisier Hotel, near Tulear, to a foyer full of foliage, pool and balconies overlooking the sea fringed soft fine white sand

– heavenly, to then be shown our individual pale stone built thatched huts with beautifully appointed rooms, just a small slope and 20 yards to our beach loungers complete with thatched parasols. We were all

down there in a short space of time and almost immediately were approached by the beach sellers with carvings and shells which we gracefully declined. Then massages were offered and taken up by two of the girls. Proven to be so good and so cheap they booked for the next day; I was now keen, at £3 for an hour's massage, even if it meant lying on a reed mat on the beach! Rob had never had a massage and was sceptical but with a little leg pulling he agreed to chance it. Having had our morning swim, dozed, read, written our diaries and repeated the motions again it was time for our session. The girls had

extremely strong hands, they took no prisoners and therefore eased away all our aches and pains, trying not to expose too much of our bodies as they anointed us with oil and reached those places which hadn't been reached for a long while! There was an "ooh" and an

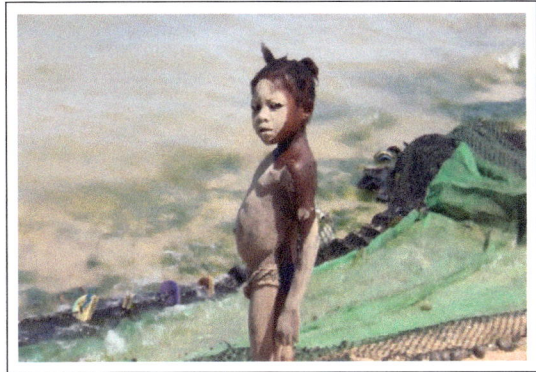

"aah" from Rob and then with such pleasure he mumbled with head still in the sand – "Our Mary, I think I am just about to purr!" He had summed up our R & R time on the beach perfectly!

I smile every time I remember our afternoon on the beach at the end of my Virginia Beach, USA friend's street. My travelling friend and I went down

for a swim and a little sunbathing with a promise of cocktails later. Enjoying a perfect afternoon, thoughts of the promise were imminent: maybe champagne along with smoked salmon type pre-

15

prandial came to mind BUT oh no, up came Anne on her bicycle complete with large wicker basket on the front. She was dressed in her shorts, chequered blouse and a large straw hat that had a gingham ribbon over the crown and over the sides of the brim, finished off with a large bow beneath her chin, making her look like someone out of *Gone with the Wind*. Braking to a halt she then 'chucked' a large packet of crisps followed by a bottle of Coca-cola. Our bubble was burst but the hilarity of the whole evening always makes us all laugh.

Yes, always a sucker for a challenge, one was set up when nearing Deception Island, an island in the South Shetlands close to Antarctica which is a caldera of an active volcano. This volcano

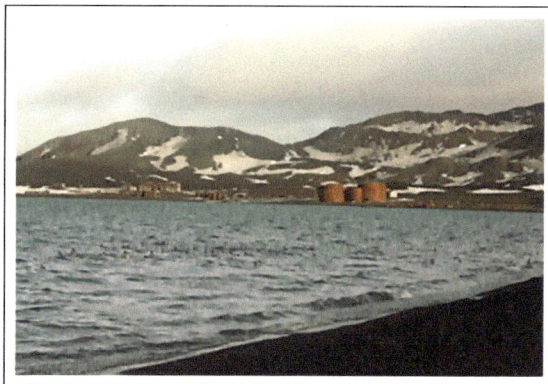

seriously damaged the local scientific stations as recently as 1967 and 1969. We could go ashore by zodiac, take our costumes and swim, and afterwards we

would receive a certificate! Bungy jumping no, but this was a challenge I just couldn't refuse. We enjoyed the most glorious sight sailing into the caldera, an enormous natural harbour, before landing on the beach by zodiac to spend a good hour wandering around

an abandoned whaling station, the old boats half buried into the beach and appreciating the flora and fauna before it was time to brace oneself for the challenge. It seemed a very good idea to leave this activity until the last when I realised getting out and back into the many layers of Antarctic gear when cold and just towelled off would be a challenge as there was still the zodiac ride back to the boat before a hot shower.

Yes indeed, in I went, with a goodly number of other passengers. I do like to swim in warm water, but this was most certainly cold, but most refreshing and great fun. We were later presented with our certificates for Antarctic Swimming, though my

friends might well say that I should have been certified years ago – while the local penguins would probably reply that there was no discussion to that fact!

Chapter 2
Childhood and Skiing

During harvest time when our fathers who were farmers were so busy, my mother took me on holiday with my 'aunt', Dad's best man's wife and their son. My first memory of travelling dates from then, on what my mother certainly thought was not the best start. It was the day before we were to leave for the Trouville Hotel, Sandown, the Isle of Wight, that Mum noticed hair floating down past the dining room window – yes, aged about five, I had found a pair of scissors and had decided that my hair needed cutting. I remember well sitting at my bedroom windowsill dropping clumps of my dark locks out of the window. Oh dear, I was required to wear a sunhat or knitted beret throughout our whole trip, so embarrassed was my poor mother!

I and my friend, one day younger than me, were always put to bed early with a glass of milk and a biscuit while Mum and Aunt went down to dinner. Needless to say, I didn't always stay put; one evening I was preparing for the next day by clambering up into the wardrobe to choose my clothes – catastrophe, over went that piece of furniture onto the end of the metal bed frame, the mirror on the door smashed, no doubt alarming the hotel maid who came into the room to find me stuck inside. During one such holiday I remember getting myself locked in the ballroom's ladies' toilet, but why I was in there, who knows? Suffice to say, I had to clamber beneath the door to escape!

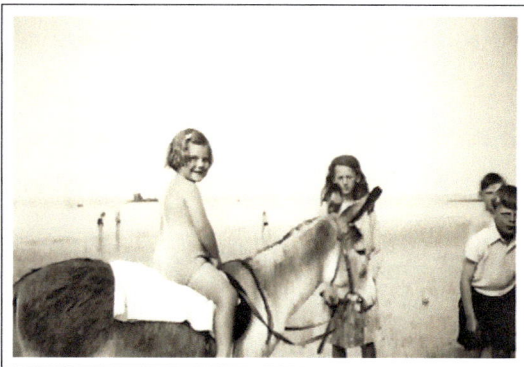

18

A few years later when I was still young, my father had a friend whose son was to compete for the Army at the services bobsleigh competitions in St Moritz, Switzerland and along with others was invited to form a support party. Dad, who had never skied and was in his late 40s, decided that we should go as a family. He rang my headmistress to ask if he could take me out of school for a fortnight (a very small convent boarding school). Her reply was instantaneous; "Yes, of course Mr. Wheildon, travel is the best education possible." Those were the days – was this where the seed of my love of travel was sown? That holiday was the beginning of decades of skiing trips, escapades and catastrophes, but more later! I was so unhappy though, that the authorities wouldn't allow me to have a go on the bobsleigh, for at 14 I was apparently too young. I was determined but had to be patient to fulfil that wish.

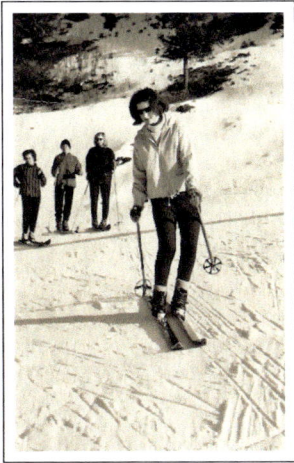

Those first ski trips were something else, rarely did we reach the top of the mountain when being lifted by an eight abreast T-bar as no one was the same height: legs, skis and arms went in all directions! Skis were measured by putting your arm as high as you could and that was the length of the ski required. Boots were all leather, fitted onto the ski with a spring at the heel and a lever at the front to tighten it all up. Certainly, there were no safety bindings in those days; rarely a day went by when a ski didn't pass us on its lonely way off piste!

We had so much fun on ski trips year after year in many different resorts and there was nearly always a drama for either the group or just myself. Missing the last lift to the top of the mountain to get home in the next valley and having to climb up the mountainside sometimes in the dark; getting lost and having to ski along tracks, again in the dark, with just the sparks from the metal beneath our skis as a guide, were common occurrences. Our front man may have had no idea where he was going anyway!

One trip a decision was made to have a barbecue right on the top of a mountain, each with part of the 'set up' in our day sack including the metal barbeque, charcoal, lighter-fluid, steaks, cutlery, buns, sauce etc. Once the fantastically scenic position was decided upon, we unpacked it all, only to find *no* matches. So next, plan B, the one who drew the short straw had to ski to the restaurant down the mountain to acquire the necessary lucifer, take the lift again and then ski across to us. After that, we all enjoyed ourselves enormously.

After lunching at a restaurant in Brévier, near Tignes and Val D'Isère, a friend and I sat on the moving chair lift, only for the assistant with a roguish glint in his eyes to give us a darn good push from behind. By then at a pretty good height, out we came into a heap in the snow beneath the next pair. That old boy was well pleased with his act, and I was grateful to have missed the rocks and the point of one of the four flailing skis!

The desire to go down that bobsleigh run stayed with me, so when I was heading for 40, I knew I must go soon otherwise they might well tell me that I was too old! I chose the resort that year and on arrival was straight down to the club to book in. My dear friends knew that they would never hear the end of it unless they too signed up, so the four of us had the experience of a lifetime. Two of us were paired with the Italian four-man bobsleigh team; we came 8th on the day and were given a certificate!

Hang-gliding wearing skis was another challenge; on a whim I decided to have a go off the top of the mountain down to the Lake in Tignes, yes, in tandem, the only problem being the wait while the professional had his lunch – I bought a brandy! But I thoroughly enjoyed the experience as indeed did the others; we had another go when we were in St Moritz.

One of our party apparently always regretted not having the 'bottle' to hang-glide and it was years later that I asked him, again on a whim, whether he would come with me in a hot-air balloon over Cappadocia. This time

he needed little persuasion! We were up and out before sunrise to clamber into the basket and with envelope fully inflated we were very quickly off over the ancient and stunning landscapes of lunar terrain that Cappadocia provides. We were both ecstatic especially when our landing was extremely gentle.

There is no way I would ever do a bungee jump, but the first time I ventured to a zip wire was an extraordinary experience. Having climbed up a simple wooden ladder strapped to the tree trunk

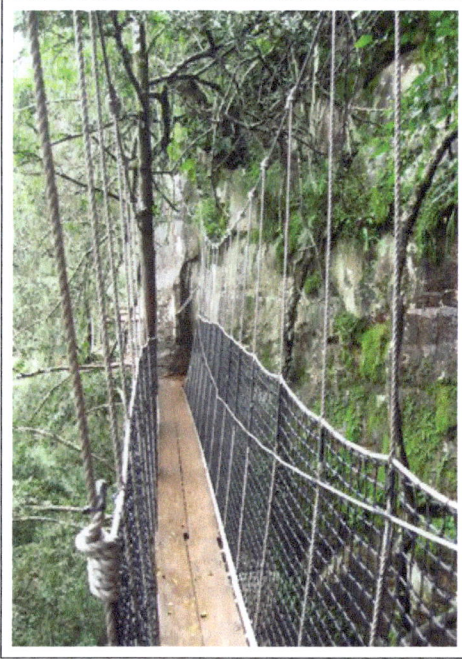

in Costa Rica and clambered onto the platform it took me quite a few minutes to brace myself for take-off. This was the most wonderful experience and went well until I had to walk the rope bridge. I reached halfway and completely froze, there was no way I could make either foot go forward, the weirdest sensation I have to say, but in time and with much encouragement there was no stopping me. Arriving at the end, I could willingly have gone straight back to the beginning for another go. Another chance came our way in the Drakensberg Mountains to take the zip wire over the canyon. That too was tremendous fun although I would love to have had a go on the Penrhyn wire over the old Welsh slate quarry, even though I am not sure whether I still have the bottle to travel at 125 mph – but then I did go down that bobsleigh run with all those corners, so come on Mary don't be ridiculous: watch this space!

Chapter 3
Transport

What do you say when you are collected by a taxi to go to the airport and the driver shows you a small Coke bottle which he is going to fill at the nearest petrol selling stall – not garage? I was completely dumb struck as he then proceeded to pour the contents down a pipe found in the glove pocket right in front of me. By then we were in the back streets and had no idea whether we were nearing our destination or not! That was Madagascar where the means of transport was most certainly diverse. We travelled on bullock carts and met many during our travels, not to mention the colourful pousse-pousse which was a glorified trolley for transporting anyone or thing including our luggage, and their own style of rickshaws, very few of which were motorized, but always lined up, keen for a fare.

On skiing trips during my youth, I

found myself coming down the mountain by the emergency method, namely the blood wagon, more than once – truthfully three times! One is so grateful, but the leg pulling never does go away – what are friends for? One flight back, once again in a wheelchair, this time in one with a flat tyre: why me, thank you very much – it was like that 'left-handed mountain' one was always looking for, as the right turn wasn't so good!

On another occasion, still amongst the snow, I arrived in Finnmark, northern Norway to stay in the Ice Hotel near Kirkenes, before travelling to Eagle Lake, which is true Sámi country. Here we were introduced to the experience of walking with snowshoes. Well, that was something else; I obviously had put mine on incorrectly as I appeared to be walking pigeon-toed and with great difficulty. But once corrected and into the rhythm we trudged like Good King Wenceslas across the lake. Before reaching the far side, we did *try* to learn the art of ice fishing; first using a giant ice screw before dropping the baited line down the hole and then waiting for the ice-char or trout to bite, happily, some did.

The next day we were challenged twice, first on being introduced to our sledges and the dogs that would pull us. Once set up, which was no easy job, we were off 'mushing' across the lake at a rapid speed. We had dramas when setting up, overtaking, with dogs fighting, anchors getting stuck, dogs pulling sledges in wrong directions and finally, trying to put the dogs into their designated

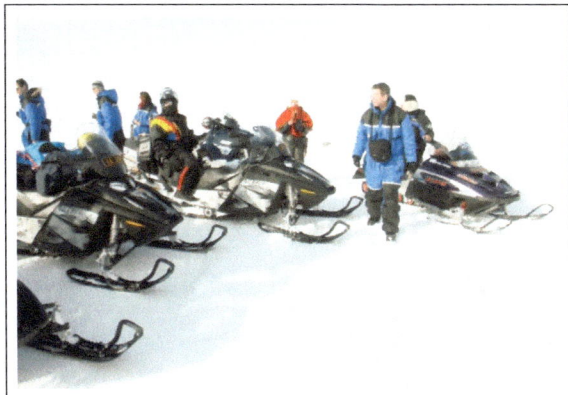

kennels – all far easier said than done!

Second was our biggest learning curve of all and I am not sure whether we ever did gain even amateur status! Having spent the night in igloo style pods at Polmac, very near the Russian border, we returned to Tana Bru some 20 miles away to be introduced to our skidoos. They would be our transport while supporting the Sámi with their herd of reindeer on the migration from Winter to their Summer pastures.

We were put through our driving drill and then we set off in pairs slowly and slightly precariously down and onto the River Tanu, which was so beautiful, but it seemed surreal to find ourselves driving along the frozen river.

Once on our way with the herd, we were to travel across the bleakest but pristine and most beautiful landscape, through glorious silver birch woodland as well as up and down many a hillside incurring many a spill while mostly off piste. We became

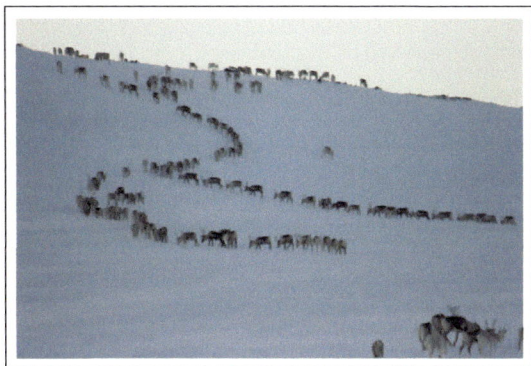

experts at righting the machines, digging ourselves out of drifts and gullies; it was all an enormous and challenging expedition. On our arrival at the North Cape lands five days later, where the herd would Summer, we were given a fun display by Kora, our mentor and many times saviour, of the real handling of these enormous machines. He was supreme.

Sitting astride that magnificent machine somehow reminds me of journeys by elephant, camel and even ostrich. One can only laugh at oneself for getting into such situations, but I can never resist a challenge! A ride on the back of an elephant usually entails climbing up a large set of steps to be at the correct level to either sit astride or onto a box frame to travel sideways – the latter I found very strange. A camel is an unusual creature, whether a dromedary, the single-humped camel, or the Bactrian, the two humped camel, which I found far more comfortable with a hump fore and aft to hang onto and lean back against! Neither is easy to mount where hanging on for grim death is a grave necessity.

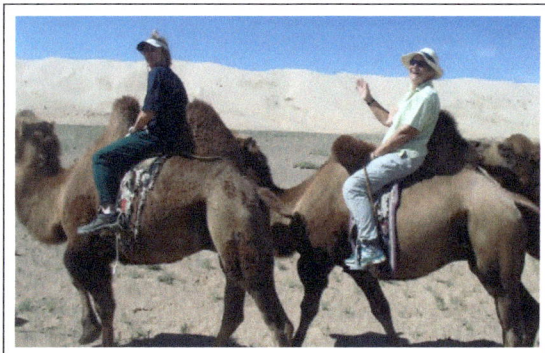

Why on earth would one wish to ride an ostrich? I cannot remember why I even said yes, perhaps now I would reply differently but I can see myself wandering up to this enormous bird in the Little Karroo, South Africa 1975, clambering up onto a fence to sit on the bird before hanging onto the poor creature's neck (or maybe it was to a rein) as we went off at a rapid speed. Memory fails me of the outcome, but I know I didn't fall off!

Although I had a pony when I was small, I was never a good rider but a friend encouraged me to join a group of her friends on their annual pony trek in Scotland. The destination that year was to ride from Glen Feshie over the Lairig Ghru, the most famous pass in Scotland with its 500m trenches that cut between the 2nd and 3rd highest mountains in the UK. Ironically, the name Lairig Ghru means debatable. It was certainly debatable whether I should have been in the group at all, but there I was having been given the most 'armchair' sized highland pony. In a line we trekked up the first mountainside and then had to dismount as the boulders were too great for the ponies – certainly with me aboard. Down and through the pass towards the River Dee we mounted once again; there were great bogs, which the ponies were so good at steering clear of and if not, getting free of – it was a true experience of an animal making the correct decisions with nature; I just hung on in wonderment.

We had encountered deer, ptarmigan and snow buntings. Finally we had to cross the river, another fine learning curve, but once the other side my trusty steed must have known exactly where he was and most certainly had the upper hand, for he was off at a canter before coming to grinding halt and deciding to have some fun with his dubious jockey. He proceeded to get down for a roll: I was out of that saddle before anyone could say: "watch out!" My glasses went flying but heyho, that was a small price. Remounted, we trundled on to beyond Marr Lodge where the ponies were boxed and taken for a full day's rest. We stayed in Braemar for two nights to enjoy a day at the Highland Games as well as to recover physically. The sounds from the telephone box shaped WC within our hotel room, as we tried to bend to go to the toilet were more than amusing – luckily we were all in the same state!

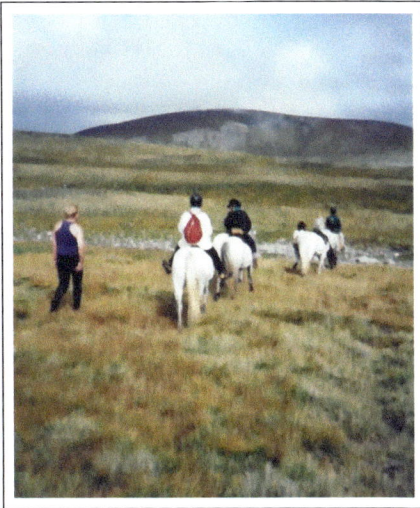

Our day in Braemar at the games was the best fun. The Royal family were there in force, it was such a lovely, relaxed event. Finally, we had to brace ourselves for the return across those fabulous mountains. We took a more southerly route which included the great gorge. Oh my, to look down that great gully left one's heart beating, but the ponies happily were so sure-footed. One stumble and that would have been cheerio! Through there, still while hanging on for life, we watched a peregrine falcon feeding its youngster in flight, a first for me: fabulous. There were ringed ouzels up there too and once down to the River Feshie we had many crossings and were overjoyed to see the dippers. Finally, a comfortable trot along the glen road took us back towards the Spey near our base at Kingussie. The Cairngorms at their best. I have since walked a slightly different route raising money for the Mountain Rescue Association up there, they do such a wonderful job.

Equally, a pair of bicycles was hired on Belle île-en-Mer, 15km off Quiberon, Brittany one very hot day for us to ride around and enjoy the beach. Sadly, for my part I disgraced myself when imbibing too much gin, with an empty stomach and the blazing sunshine – oh deary me! I also hired a bike when staying for a weekend on Sark, I came to a stinging end there that time, when going across a field to visit a friend, hitting a bump that sent me diving off the bike into the fresh spring nettles; I believe that was the last time I sat astride a bike!

Age does change a few things, I confess. The campervans we have hired have been the greatest fun. They are diverse in their size and facilities. A friend stopped us booking a van from Cairns to Brisbane as she knew there was to be an eclipse just before our requirements, so she would book us into returning a vehicle for the van company. Great, $5 a day, fuel and insurance covered but only three days to do it in.

In the end we purchased a further two days to visit Daintree Rainforest, Cape Tribulation before travelling south on our 'duty' journey. This OLD vehicle was as large as an enormous horse box and had most certainly seen better

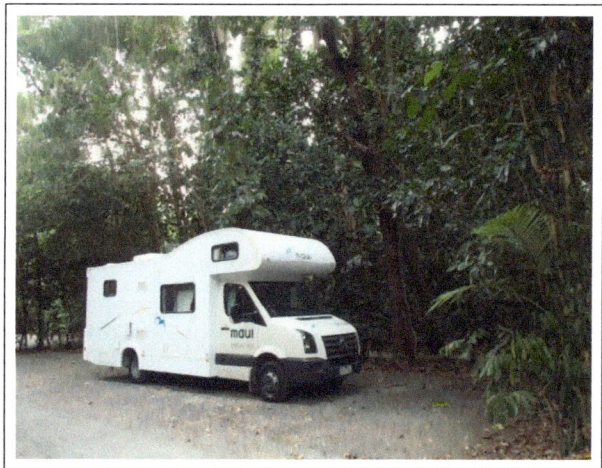

days. Learning to drive it was our immediate challenge, and to take enough road around a roundabout or sharp bend was the first initiation! Happily, we were driving back through Cairns on our southern journey so were much relieved to call in at the head office workshop to have all the doors, TV and fridge tightened up as they swung open or across the vehicle at every bend in the road – a nightmare until then.

The same dear friend, who is we all agree, very 'careful' – booked a campervan for our week in Tasmania. Having been just the two of us in that great horsebox, we were now four in what was no more than a converted 'white van man's van'. Two of us were not small, the others were slim; there we were, with just three seats upfront, and no facilities except the minimum kitchen requirements. A double bed was resplendent below and what I would consider to be an overhead shelf for the other two. Reaching this meant placing a foot on the kitchen surface before bending double and sideways to slide in; then you had to struggle into the sleeping bag before creeping into the far corner while the second maneuvered into the spare space and into their bag. A nightmare for them, a darn good laugh for the two of us below. It is truly amazing how the mind rides over matter as none of us needed to get out in the night that week, but we all agreed that by 6am we acted like well-shaken champagne bottles and were out of that tiny vehicle with great speed to the block provided.

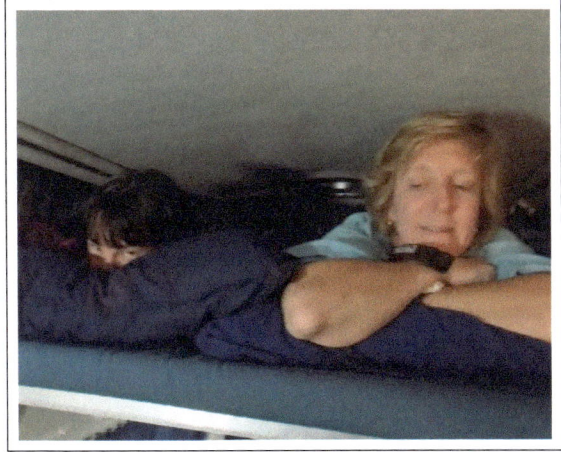

Campervans are generally trouble-free but this second one decided to die on us at Campbell Town during the Christmas holidays, (a town where many convicts were sent). The hire company was on skeleton staff, so it took them quite a long while to get a maintenance man to us. Happily the town we were in proved most interesting, so we whiled away our time easily rather than feel 'convicted' ourselves. As once on safari,

the cause was the battery connection – again under the passenger seat. Extraordinary!

At the end of October 1967, I ventured on an epic train journey, leaving Newport News, Virginia with a reel of tickets that was well over a yard long: northwards to Detroit, Buffalo, Windsor and Toronto to catch the Canadian National, complete with panoramic lounge to travel across Canada to Vancouver. What a fabulous journey, as it proved to be until near Golden where, with a big bump, we came off the rails. There we were in the middle of the mountainside but not in the slightest worried, no one was hurt; we were already having a ball, I had met such fun people; the party simply continued with the added provision of free food for the rest of the journey. We were held up for about 24 hours while the rail was 'mended' and the carriages put back onto the track. I have since returned to Banff and Lake Louise and discovered a sign to Golden – memories!

In Vancouver I stayed with the family of a fellow I had met on the train, who took me out to Grouse Mountain and also down to the river where surprise-surprise he just continued on into that river. I hadn't realised I was in an amphibian! My onward journey took me from Vancouver to San Francisco and then back across the USA via Salt Lake City and finally Newport News taking a full six weeks. Memories of sleeping overnight on a station bench, visiting friends in Edmonton, distant family in Calgary and actually only staying for one night in a youth hostel in San Francisco remain joyous, otherwise it was travel friends, or their friends' floor or sofa. Such is travel, transport and the camaraderie!

That train journey across Canada was wonderful but the journey from Cusco to Machu Picchu was simply amazing. We had to be at the San Pedro station at 7am as the journey on the

Ferrocarril Santa Ana took four hours. It is a 3ft narrow gauge line, which boasts a series of five switchbacks locally known as 'El Zig-Zag' which enabled the train to climb up the steep incline out of the imperial city, passing through a chaos of streets and shacks which clung precariously to the hillside. There was only one engine, Canadian, either pushing or pulling Japanese railcars: hence very narrow seats! The train ran alongside the River Pomatates for a period before descending 6,500ft to the River Urubamba. The Incas called it the Wilka Mayo, meaning sacred river and of course it runs into the Sacred Valley and is the largest tributary of the Amazon. The train went alongside the Inca trail and passed the Inca Suspension Bridge.

We saw the snow-peaked Mount Veronica at 19,00ft, and organ pipe cactuses growing – we learned that the Incas used the cactus fibre for rope making. We had been primed to leave our seats to be beside the door 20 minutes before the

arrival time because there would be an enormous rush for the few buses that would take us to Macchu Picchu itself. The four full hours we spent there were simply incredible, and with relatively few people around the vast area we could wander at our will. Back on those hard train seats was somewhat tedious but we had enjoyed a most memorable day, learned so much and experienced a very different type of train transport!

Moving to watery recollections; many times have I waited for the Skye ferry at Kyle of Lochalsh and Armadale, enjoying the experience of going on those drive on, drive off ferries to the Inner and Outer Hebrides. As we were sailing out of Glasgow, with friends on their 32ft yacht, towards Bute, they kindly gave me the wheel; I was going fine and quite content until suddenly, after checking behind, I realised the steamer *Waverley* was gaining on us at a rapid rate. In panic, I immediately handed over my duties. But what a great looking boat she is. Later, during the same trip sailing out to Arran we came into strong winds – sorry, I lost about five hours of my life that afternoon. I keep trying but I do know that I am sea-sick on a lilo in a swimming pool!

Finally returning from working in Virginia, USA in 1968 and having gained so much 'stuff' I enquired about travelling home by ship. The only one leaving New York at the end of October was the *Queen Elizabeth 1*. I purchased a trunk at a junk shop which was taken by a friend living in New York to the ship. I discovered that this was that great liner's last voyage across the Atlantic to Southampton arriving on November 5th, bonfire night (actually day). What a voyage we had, rough was the word in more ways than one! Alcoholic, it was for sure. The officers bar beer tap was turned on as we left New York and was not turned off until we arrived in Southampton. Not a drop was wasted as jugs were placed beneath if there wasn't an empty beer-tankard being filled. I do not remember making breakfasts but lunched

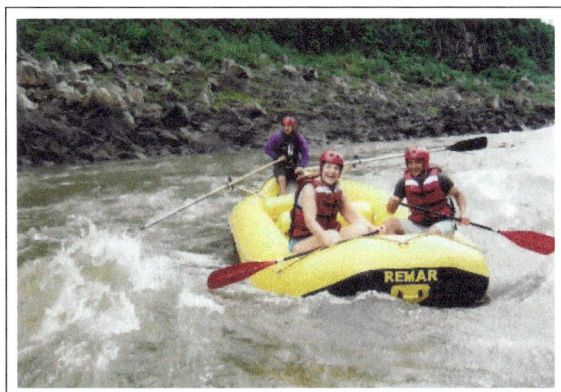

occasionally. Out on deck – well it was far too rough, certainly dangerous, but all massive fun.

A friend and I decided we would sign our lives away to take a dinghy ride beneath the falls at Iguassu. We had already visited by a more stable launch but wanted more! We must have been mad but oh my, that was some experience. We were fine until we hit some rapids that tipped the boat 90 degrees, sufficient to decant our boatman. I found myself pushed down to the front of this tiny rubber vessel; and Celia, thankfully, was still hanging on too. We managed to gather our boatman, more by luck than any ability and continued down the river to the landing stage. Will I ever learn?!

Returning one time to visit my friends in Virginia Beach I was very taken by the idea of flying by Concorde. I had seen an advert whereby one could travel very cheaply for DHL taking just hand luggage. I was up for that, flying out 747, returning from New York to London on that amazing bird. BUT my

friends at home were oh so worried that I would be taking drugs or similar, and couldn't believe it was all legal. Sadly, the schedule didn't synchronise well with my ongoing flight to Norfolk, Virginia forcing me to stay in a hotel in New York overnight. This was all before the internet, but I did find accommodation at what appeared to be an expensive hotel, but reasonably priced for the area where I needed to be. Oh my, on arrival I was convinced I had booked myself into a brothel – I hardly dare come out of my room but when I did, I left my money and passport in the cistern for safety – the price of flying by Concorde! With only hand luggage and staying with my friend at the beach, both she and I were fed up with my same outfits for over three weeks. The plane was magnificent, such comfortable leather seats, great service and what an experience. Most of the passengers beside me were businessmen but were keen for me to have a great time, I loved it.

In 1998 I was invited to travel to Bhutan with the intention of flying a hot air balloon in numerous districts of that unique kingdom. I was so excited as I had always dreamed of travelling to that Himalayan Buddhist gem, known as the Home of the Thunder Dragon. Our basket and envelope with equipment were shipped off months before to sail to India and then travel by road into Bhutan. Normally butane is used for inflating the envelope, but this was not available, so a lorry of gas cylinders was transported from India arriving just after we had reached Thimphu, the capital. We had flown to Katmandu and then into the famous steep Paro Valley, passing roofs covered in bright red drying chillies, and then finally by road to the capital.

Once the logistics of transporting the various baskets and envelopes were worked out, we were a party of 26 with six baskets, all most excited

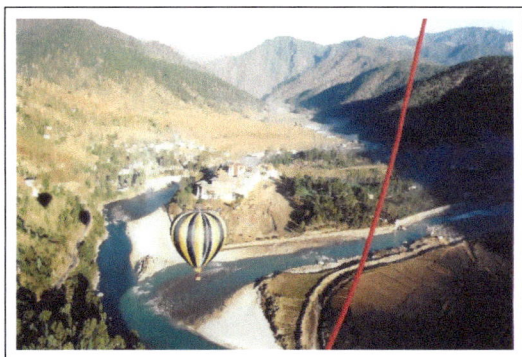

to reach our first launching point. With our allocated driver, Kado, we travelled to Punakha where we camped beside the Mo Chhu river. The valley there is quite wide, but we knew that we could not fly outside this valley as there was absolutely no infrastructure on the other side. We were also instructed that in no way were we ever to fly over the Dzongs (Monasteries).

It was truly amazing how we went up and how the winds took us up the valley, it was both incredible and exhilarating. We finally landed quite safely beside the river with a sigh of satisfaction and jubilation. The next flight took us in the opposite direction, this time immediately over the Dzong across the meeting of the Mo Chhu and the Pho Chhu rivers, a phenomenal if not *permitted* sight. We flew on trying to find a suitable landing spot but to no avail, with Kado trailing us and trying to persuade us to land on the back of his truck. He didn't understand that we were wind dependent and had to have zero wires or trees in our way.

We were finally forced to land in paddy fields beside the Mad Monks Monastery. Poor Kado was beside himself as we were so far from the road with absolutely no access at all for his vehicle. Much scratching of heads occurred and finally with a collection of strong locals and a couple of long bamboo poles to thread through the handles the basket could be carried like a sedan chair. With much huffing and puffing, it was finally lifted onto the truck bed – we were very late home to the camp site and for lunch!

We moved onto the Bumthang district, staying in Jakar. We thrilled the locals by inviting them to come to the recreation ground beside the river where we all tethered our baskets to vehicles

and gave some a ride, lifting the balloons as high as our ropes would allow.

This was only the second time that balloons had been allowed into Bhutan to fly; The Fourth King had given his permission and had also asked that all schools should teach their children about them just in case they saw them and were frightened. Most certainly, the Jakar locals were thrilled to bits.

One flight from there was interesting, we flew just where we were not supposed to again – over the Dzong; here we could simply only wave to the monks below, thankfully they appeared thrilled and waved back enthusiastically! BUT coming down to land, life was not so easy as a suitable place was just not there. In desperation we flew over to the rear of a hotel and landed in a steep field. I will never forget jumping out of the basket and trying to run up the steep field breathlessly (altitude 2,800m), which smelled glorious with the wild thyme beneath my feet trying to reach the line and save the envelope from catching on the washing lines. Oh yes, there was a little corner that caught, happily no damage was incurred but amusingly of all, the hotel belonged to the Queen of Bhutan! All was fine and for Kado, the road was nearby so not too great a carry-out that time.

Travelling further east to Ura, we camped below the farmhouse and just above the Monastery in a very large field. But further up the valley was deemed the take-off point for a flight that would permit a journey over the mountain and into the next valley. Because of the altitude and the gas requirement, it was decided that just two would fly,

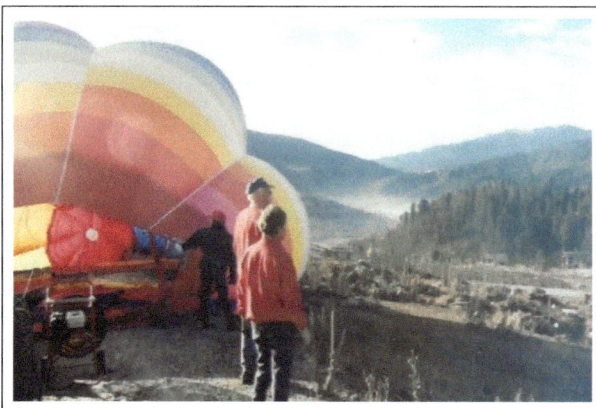

so I was on the ground. That was an incredible experience trying to keep sight of them as they went up and over, finally arriving at the other side of the mountain and being so relieved that they were again in sight. But where to land? It was my turn to be guiding them towards our trailer. Remarkably they ended up within feet of Kado's truck – his face was one of joy and jubilation or perhaps plain relief!

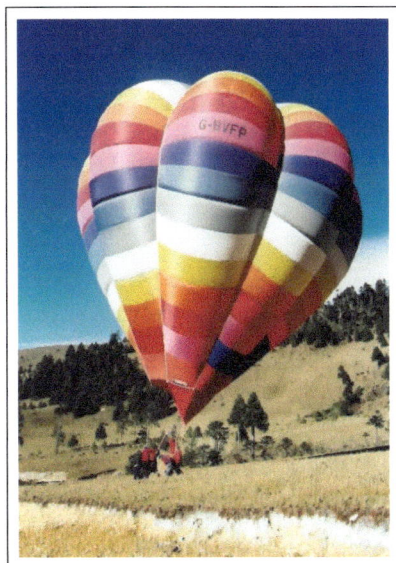

Speaking of trucks; on my very first visit to Africa (1975) I was invited to stay up at Wankie Park in Rhodesia. My friend and I were booked to go on the sunset safari drive, to then sleep up in a tree overnight before returning to our hotel after the sunrise safari. An exciting plan but as the afternoon time arrived so did a raging storm! My friend ducked, not wanting to go out in it, but having looked forward to this for so long, as well as having all the vaccinations required for Africa, I was not going to miss out. No fancy vehicle for the three of us, oh no. We had to clamber onto the bed of an open-back truck and simply hang onto the rollbar. I loved it, we saw so much game, it was just such a thrill to me until, after the sun had set, we drove into a great pit. The poachers had dug an enormous square hole covering the area with slim trunks of wood and foliage to trap an elephant who would fall in and be unable to clamber out. We were well and truly in. This of course was before any mobile phone systems. No one was hurt, so with our weapon, a machete, we had to walk to our camp and me to my tree-house bed for the night. That was my initiation to

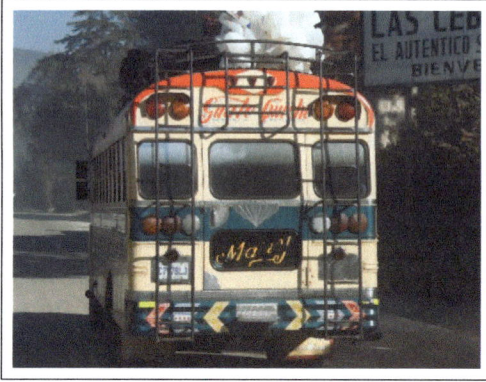

sunset safaris. My next was the sunrise safari the following morning when we obviously had to return to our hotel base. A walking safari is simply incredible, especially at dawn when herds of antelope, zebra and elephants are still dozing or just coming to. The mist was beginning to rise and the whole atmosphere was calm. I just revelled in it, but not until I arrived back at base did I think of the fact that there may have been danger, be it from the animals, reptiles, or insects. I was in an innocent's heaven!

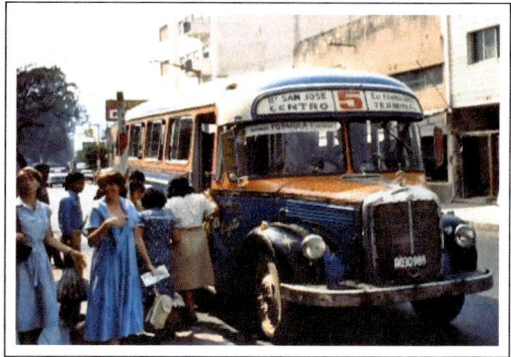

Travel and transport come in so many guises but that is what makes it so much fun – whatever, one must just keep on smiling. Journeying by coach is always a challenge, be it a superb luxury limousine or a clapped-out Indian, gaudy, smoke emitting aged bus; they come in many varieties of size and comfort.

One wooden open-sided vehicle collected us at Iquitos Airport to transport us to the Amazon to catch our small boat back in 1980. The locals were around us like locusts, some children offering us a two-toed sloth which

I will never forget.

Another on Hiva Oa in the Marquesas Islands also acted as the school bus, again wooden, with a straight bench down either side and another up the middle that we sat astride.

My trip from Tahiti to the Tuamotu Atolls and then on to the Marquesas Islands was unique. Planning my Silver Gap trip around the world had taken me a year with great guidance from Adrian of Trailfinders. I needed to travel from New Zealand to San Francisco; I had been invited to Colombia and Uruguay but the flight costs to South America from New Zealand were astronomical,

so this thought was abandoned. I did mention that I had always wanted to go on a banana boat and also to the South Sea Atolls. Adrian was immediately on the case, he knew of the *Aranui 3*, a Chinese cargo ship that took passengers on its two-week trip every three weeks. It is basically the Tuamotu Atolls and Marquesas Islands corner shop. This accommodation was just what I wanted except for the price for a cabin plus the dreaded single supplement. However, he continued, there were dormitories aboard; these appeared to be within my 'Silver Gap bracket' and having been to a boarding school I thought no more about signing up for it. On arrival, I was advised where to find my 'dormitory' – oh glory be. Error of all errors.

However, thankfully every cloud has a silver lining. I arrived in this approximately 9ft square 'dormitory' which had double bunks on four sides, each 6ft long. The remainder was two lots of four shelves, one set of eight drawers and a door. Not so much as a chair or table and certainly not a single porthole! I was on the top bunk and there was no way I would have been able to sit upright or share my space with enough luggage for 101 days! It was mixed and the others were French, not that I was too worried about that, but the last straw was finding that there were two other similar dormitories besides who shared the three toilets, three basins and three showers! I was out of there and back up to the reception before you could say "where is my credit card"! Yes, indeed, I could upgrade but it was suggested I might well have to share with an islander between islands. My 'state room' was marvellous. I had a spare bed to put all my paperwork and camera stuff on, my own shower room and WC, dressing table and a glorious window. I didn't pay that dreaded single supplement and I never did have to share!

Wow, what a ship, that was the most wonderful trip – meeting up with fabulous people, enjoying the navigational abilities of the great seamen of the South Sea Islands and their famous tattoos. How did they manoeuvre the boat into the narrowest of channels, turn it, anchor it or if there was a pier, tie it up? Never once did you hear a voice, it was all done by signs. The downloading was sometimes by a whale boat (flatbed raft), sometimes by small boat and then on occasion, onto the shoulders of a helper out in the water. The variety of goods delivered was diverse. First the post and then possibly a tray of eggs, a whole Brie, a new canoe, light bulbs, fridge, tractor or maybe just beer! Uploading included their mail – which might include their wonderful pearls, as well as copra, manoi, empty fuel drums and of course any rubbish.

Interestingly, the islanders had to order and pay for their goods 10 days before the ship sailed and these goods were then ticked off the delivery sheet on collection. All very swift and businesslike.

Another form of transport to challenge us was a quad bike. Jack's Camp in the Makgadikgadi Salt Pans (Botswana/Namibia border) was just building Planet Baobab, providing a more economical camp (I now learn that has been voted one of the top 10 most extraordinary places to stay in the world by Lonely Planet) however, we were paying only 50% as I was to write an article on the new venue!

Once nearing the camp, we parked under the ancient baobab trees and by way of direction arrows, made from beer and Coca-Cola cans, as well as the sound of steel band music, we found an African lady skimming cow dung onto a brand new Kalunga Hut. This region is the baobab capital of

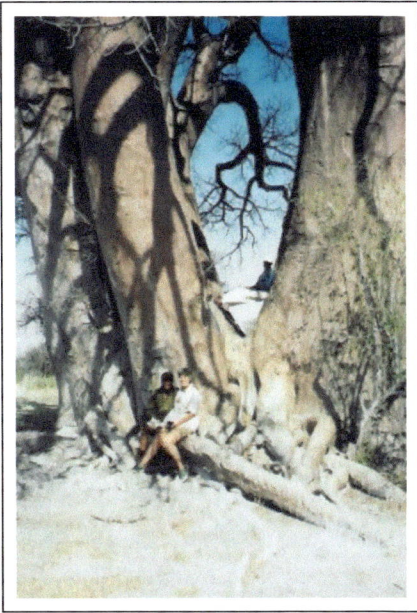

the world where the average tree is more than 4,000 years old. We loved our one night there and also our night sleeping under the stars in the pan itself but we were away early the next morning, first to visit a huge 6,000-year-old baobab tree carved with lots of initials and dates. Our guides told us that David Livingstone

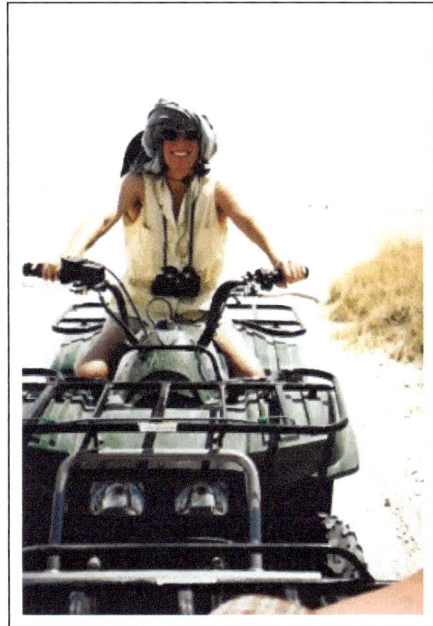

used to leave messages in a large hole in the trunk where they could be collected.

We continued onto Jack's Camp to be introduced to our quad bikes! Our heads were wrapped in a cloth called a 'keykuise' and with minimum instructions we mounted our machines and were off in a long snaking line across the salt pans in mounting heat and dust. That was true fun, but oh my, we were in a very dusty state when we arrived back at Jack's Camp, in time for a basic shower, that being water from a bag above our heads, and the well-earned lunch!

Where no post office transport is required is the unique post box at Post Office Bay, on Floreana Island, Galápagos. Yes, we had to have a go at leaving cards in there for both ourselves and for friends, though we did not chance Livingstone's tree-hole! A few were back in a couple of weeks, whilst one took 17 years and some never came! The idea was that you 'fertled' amongst the post and took home what you could personally deliver.

By the by, whichever method of transport, whatever the map or GPS says, some signs will be there to give you confidence, or doubt, or simply a darn good laugh. This one was found in New Zealand, a country whose inhabitants are always full of fun and very happy to advise the best route. Happy travelling.

Chapter 4
Road Conditions

One can but smile at the thought, when just walking up the high street of our own local conurbation, how easy it is to trip on uneven paving and if falling, to miss an ongoing car, or whether to hold back or get soaked whilst roadside on a wet day as vehicles head for that large puddle beside you. Over the world the weather most certainly takes its toll; rain causing landslides, surfaces being cracked dramatically or simply washed away. Wind causes trees to fall, snow, sand and water to be driven across the road surface, and hard frosts and extreme heat add to the havoc.

A cousin of mine took on the ultimate challenge to my mind when competing in, and, I hasten to add, winning, the London to Sydney Vintage Car Endurance Trial (1987), choosing to cross the Sahara north to south – I didn't realise and neither did they that most of that desert lies in Algeria, into which you could drop the whole of Australia and quite a lot of the sea around it! From the southern end of the Sahara, they headed southeast to Mombasa with no support system whatsoever. From there they reached Perth, Australia and continued right across the Nullabar to Sydney. They had built their own standard 30s Talbot from a pile of bits gleaned over two years. My experiences have been not quite so extreme!

Ethiopia was interesting in many ways but the roads, oh my! We drove out of Addis Ababa, which like any third-world city was filled with stinking vehicles, fumes, animals, and people. Despite the hazards very soon we were

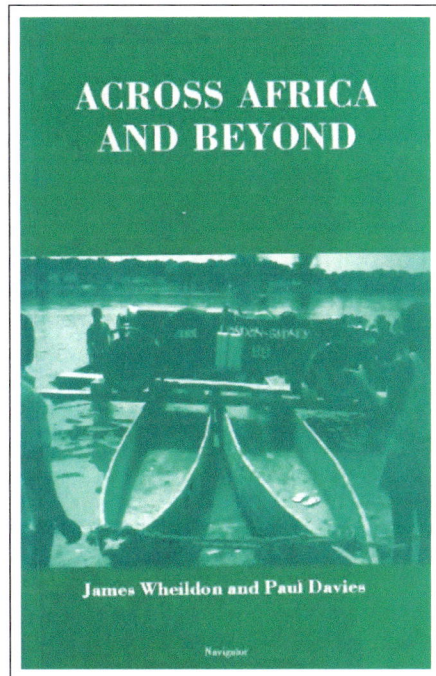

ACROSS AFRICA
AND BEYOND

James Wheildon and Paul Davies

Navigator

on the open road heading to Awassa. There followed 70 miles upon relatively good tar to Debre Zeit where we dropped down into the Rift Valley and said goodbye to that surface until the end of our trip. Thankfully we had a superb guide and exceptional driver complete with an ex-UN land cruiser.

Letting us down gently we travelled on newly upgraded roads for a further 50 miles through Shashamane and onto Awassa. Reality hit the next day as we climbed into the hills; the views, the beauty, the wildlife and the continuous trail of people kept us sane as the roads became dire. Thank goodness for our driver and Land cruiser. Dodola, Dinsho and Robe were three of the villages we passed on our way to Goba. It took us six hours encountering one motorbike, two trucks and one bus other than a continuous train of donkeys, goats, cattle, horses and poultry with families going to and from their local village market – we now understood why the need for tarmac was certainly not great!

Spending a day upon the Sanetti Plateau and Harenna Escarpment was fabulous, but the road was so poor! Did it matter when we could enjoy 13 sightings of the Ethiopian wolf, the rarest canid in the world, rare giant mole-rats, blue-winged geese, Abyssinian hare and even klipspringer? Many a time we were out shifting boulders to make a better track. Sitting beside the driver I tried to decide which would be my best route, glad all the while he was making the choices! Whether steep, either up or down, wet or dry, it was hair-raising but often, hiding white knuckles, we laughed. Amazingly it was on our last night before returning to Addis that we

endured our only break – a busted spring. Previously we had suffered only one flat tyre. Our guide and driver went off into the night, returning the next morning with what he considered as the 'mended' spring. Rob, our agricultural mechanical companion, gave it the official check, considered 'bodged' was more the task's proper report. However, with much TLC we returned to Addis safely.

The infrastructure in Madagascar is hardly fluid, so we found ourselves repeatedly flying back to the capital Antananarivo locally known as 'Tana', and then on to yet another area of that enormous island to be met by a sad mixture of vehicles which were required to transport us over even sadder surfaces! Like Ethiopia, the usual transport was on foot, but here with added donkey cart, simple wooden hand-pushed cart, 'pousse pousse' (a cross between a Chinese rickshaw and an Indian phut-phut) or ox wagon, but very few bicycles. With the combination of our provided vehicles and the bumpy pot-holed road surfaces we enjoyed a pretty shaky trip, to say the least!

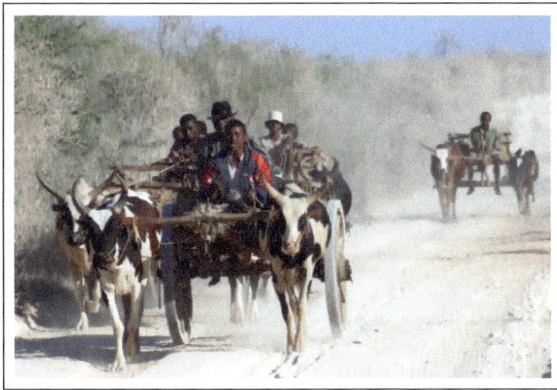

Namibia was totally different as we had our marvellous long-based Land Rover to self-drive over thousands of miles of corrugated roads. We found that a steady 60mph gave us the most comfortable ride; the roads were incredibly straight with a mirage beyond most of the time, so keeping

an eye out for a big dip, hump or sudden animal was relatively easy, but I must admit, extremely wearing.

Not always was it thus because one needs to go into the sand dunes, onto beaches, and around game parks

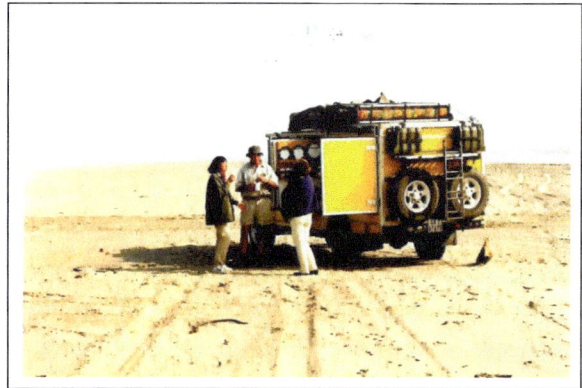

all of which provide their own challenges. Yes, we occasionally became stuck but with diff lock and tyre pressures let down, somehow, we always extricated ourselves. Weather is generally the biggest provider of difficult driving conditions in the game parks, so care is always necessary and yes, we certainly had our hair-raising moments!

We were so lucky to spend a month in Chile, an incredibly long country. Compare the top of Norway down to Morocco and turn that upside down,

that is Chile, never wider than 300 miles: quite remarkable. We enjoyed amazing journeys across the altiplano of the Atacama Desert, across salt flats with bearable if tiring bumpy surfaces. Towns were good and further south driving down part of the famous Carretera Austral from Coyhoique to El Pangue the surface was wonderful.

The Transpantaneira in Brazil was yet another challenge. Work had started in 1971 to construct a road across

the Pantanal, it would start at Poconé and finish at Corumbá, 211 miles away. Sadly, work had stopped after 100 miles at Porto Jofre on the Cuiabá River and has never continued. For the construction, earth was excavated which formed two ditches either side of the roadbed. These ditches became canals continuously filling with water, producing excellent fish habitat and attracting their predators. Due to the enormous quantity of water 125 wooden bridges had to be built, many of

which by the time we arrived in 2011 were in a pretty sad state. However, when we arrived at 'Mile 10' in a highly suitable vehicle, any suffering of discomfort along the straight murram track was allayed by the teeming wildlife on both sides. We continued to cross 'bridge after bridge' in questionable condition, spotting more and more birds, caiman, capybara and even the Pantaneiro driving their cattle along the road.

Travelling the roads in India means nothing but traffic, traffic and more traffic over surfaces that are generally in extremely poor repair once out of the main conurbations. Driving overnight from Bombay (Mumbai) Airport south along the main road to India's National Defence Academy at Khadakwasla, Pune, was a nightmare. The road was filled with trucks of enormous size, many overloaded, with no lights, broken down or travelling on the wrong side of the road. We were in a taxi with no idea of where we were and were terrified, sitting in the back being thrown up and down, this way and that. Never have I been more pleased to arrive at our destination, even when the duty guard knew nothing of our expected arrival.

The road from Darjeeling up to Sikkim was another similar journey – horrendous. This time with far greater hills as well as narrowing roads; we travelled by traditional taxi to Pemayangtse (2085m) near Pelling, Sikkim some 110km west of Gangtok. Oh, glory be, that was a rattling experience where we simply had to grin and bear it for the glories of the view and the villages en route to

our destination. Once there, we had to keep laughing at our experiences for our hotel was the coldest ever. One night at that hostelry – diarised as The Hotel from Hell, was one night too many, but we wouldn't have missed the visit for the world as the views and the monastery, the oldest in Sikkim, were simply wonderful – it was the price we had to pay!

The road from Bagdogra to Phuentsholing, the border town of Bhutan, must be the worst ever. One immediately hears horns and cringes at the sight ahead as the vehicle dodges oncoming cars, bicycles, trucks, buses, cows, rickshaws and people. The surface went from bad to worse as we travelled through the Darjeeling tea plantations towards the Teesta River and the Coronation Bridge, and nothing improved at all as we bumped our way beside the Bengal tea plantations within the Duars, the Himalayan foothills. Thank goodness for the roof of our bus over those four hours, for I believe we might have had a shortage of passengers if it had not been there!

Bhutan is a whole different story. It was only in the 60s that the King invited India to help build roads within his kingdom. Tamils came to lay the first

paved road, which opened in 1961, they are still there continuing the work. Phuentsholing, one of only two entries into the country, stands at 100ft above sea level but from that point it is uphill, with an average of 17 bends

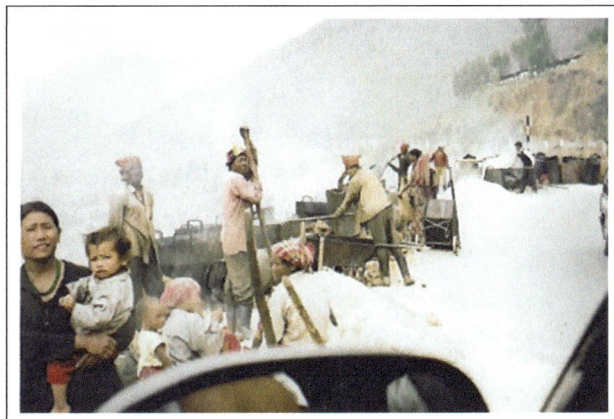

to every kilometre. Zigzagging up one hillside over the pass only to zigzag the other side down to a river is the norm. Added to that are the drops to the valley, which are beyond comprehension and rarely have any form of barrier. Rarely also, the sound of a horn, but the traffic is not heavy. Known as the Home of the Thunder Dragon because of the enormous storms caused by the Himalayan Mountain range there are often serious landslides, generally because of the huge waterfalls that form near or on a bend thus requiring tremendous road and bridge maintenance. We met many serious problems, so at times we would walk through the slide while the driver took the bus gently across the dangerous track. Happily, the drivers I have been blessed with have been brilliant, though in fact, then, one could not self-drive within Bhutan unless on a special licence. They cared greatly for their vehicles, taking the smoothest route which everyone of us appreciated as we swayed from 'cheek to cheek' and swung around each bend praying that there wasn't someone doing the same in the opposite direction!

In Australia cousin Jude and I were once again travelling in a glorious campervan. Wonderful roads even when we travelled onto the rural routes, but life wasn't always hunky-dory. Sometimes there were signs that said soft sand: this was so as we travelled from Badgingarra, hit the Brand Highway before turning off westwards onto the Jurien Way East and that is where *catastrophe* hit us. I had been so thrilled to spot a new plant and then around the corner another – forgetting the earlier 'beware soft sand' sign – I drove off the tarmac onto what I thought was a layby, oh deary me. The harder I tried, the deeper the wheels dug in. I was stuffed! As always, very little traffic appeared, but in due course a 4x4 came by and continued around the corner *BUT* happily they returned and offered us help which resulted in our immediate extrication!

I have always preferred reading travel books to fiction, perhaps since reading *Desert Taxi* when I was just 14. Subsequently, I have longed to go to the Gobi Desert and see it for myself. In August 2017 four of us arrived at the Chinggis Khaan International Airport, Ulaanbaatar, to travel by 4x4 over the steppe, the great grasslands and the Karakoram of Mongolia. Oh my, that was out in a 'never-never' land, I was in my element. We travelled for five days without one sign of tarmac, crossing through rivers many times (never a bridge) – we certainly quickly

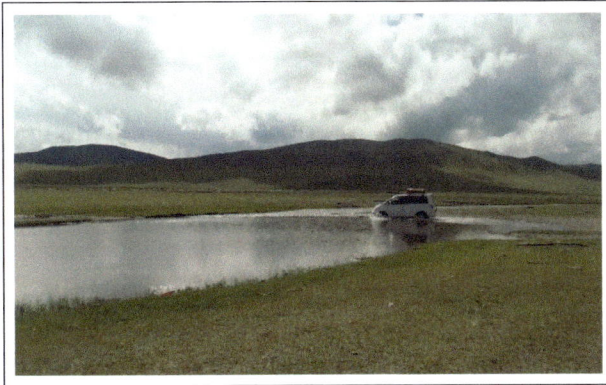

learned the reason for the periscope-style exhausts! We crossed miles of flat lands – it is no wonder some people thought the world was flat; but we also clambered through rocky and sandy terrain and simply across 'green lands' which were certainly not grass as we know it, but mostly alliums and wildflowers. Sensational.

Road conditions when one travels on 'expedition' type trips are par for the course and without a sense of humour life would be hopeless. Jumping out of our vehicle to help put enough planks across a bridge or gully before travelling across, what can one do but laugh and live in hope? One road we were definitely not able to travel across was when we disembarked from our icebreaker at Iqaluit, Canada's northernmost city. During the night before our arrival a car had burned out, on the very road we were to take from the quay into town. As a result, the permafrost had melted and produced an enormous hole across the width of the route. Iqaluit, we learned, has the 3rd highest tide differential (15.5 metres) so instead of a comfortable bus ride from the quayside to the airport we had to disembark from ship to zodiac, then from our zodiac into the shallows for a very wet landing! Before our very eyes the tide was receding at an extremely rapid rate as we proceeded to slip and slide through boulders and wrack carrying our hand luggage to the beach where we most inelegantly had to leave our borrowed wellingtons, life jackets and wet weather gear. Hardly ocean liner stuff!

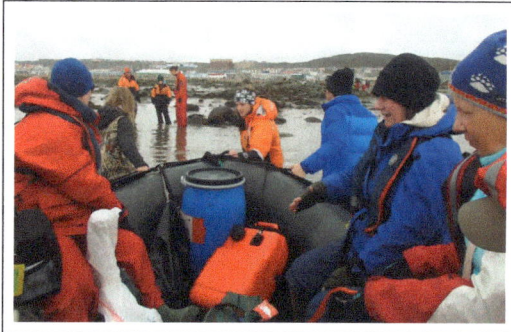

Finally, I have the never-to-be-forgotten memory of our small coach travelling across Tibet where the road surfaces were never good, so much so that our brave driver often chose to drive along the riverbed for a more direct route. This route appeared to be the norm in November when we were journeying, with the rivers having a little more than a trickle so were easily crossed. Was the surface smooth? Most certainly not, and dusty, oh glory be. We were forced to travel with scarves wrapped around our faces most of the time. At some of the landslides we were required to form a gang of 'rock clearers', to allow us to daringly proceed. Our luggage which was either stored in the open undercarriage or up on the roof was regularly in a dire state when we arrived at our evening destination. There was never the opportunity to have that longed-for shower before putting on clean clothes, but none of us would have changed a thing for the beauty of the land and the friendliness of the Tibetans.

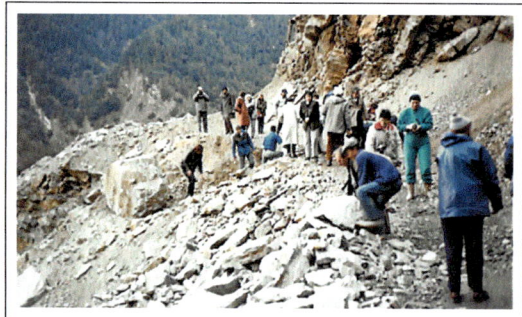

Chapter 5
Airports: Airline Dramas

My first flight was in 1953, the year of Queen Elizabeth II's Coronation when Mum and I were on holiday with her friend and son on the isle of Jersey. We flew to Dinard for the day in a tiny plane that was oh so exciting for us all. My experiences of airports since that day, their sizes and differences, are as wide as one could ever imagine.

One of my most vivid memories is of an early flight which recalls the problem of cologne continuously dripping from the luggage rack onto my head. No one could find the source, and with no other seat available, it simply continued to dampen me! Another time involved a bottle of red wine being accidentally poured by the hostess over my light-coloured skirt at the beginning of a long-haul flight, causing me to have to spend the rest of the journey wrapped in an airline blanket while the washed skirt dried out.

Yet another memory concerns my absolute amazement at seeing a local fellow along the row pumping up his 'gaz' stove with saucepan above, heating his maté on a flight from Bolivia to Peru; who could imagine that these days? Maté is a traditional South American caffeine-rich infused drink. It is made by soaking dried leaves of the holly species, *Ilex paraguariensis*, in hot water and is served with a metal straw in a container typically made from a calabash gourd. Yes, we had smoking on board then too, but now his actions seem totally beyond comprehension. Equally a flight within China was hair-raising. We waited patiently at the airport sitting on long pew-like wooden benches each with a 'potty' at the end. This I soon learned was a spittoon. But once aboard I was given a canvas seat with no belt: heyho!

In Petropavlovsk, Kamchatka Peninsula, Eastern Russia we were bussed from our boat to the Avachinsky heliport, allocated our tickets out on the tarmac, before being hastened to a huge MI-8 army machine standing out on the helipad ready for our one hour flight. Once seated, belted and with earmuffs on, it was time for final instructions. First, we flew over farmland before the beginning of the volcanic mountain range. The gigantic helicopter flew right around the Karymsky volcano, then the Maly Semyachik volcano, where the acidic lake within shone spectacularly. The colour was caused by 'pure acid': hydrochloric and sulphuric. The volcano was steaming away as we circled first one side and then the next and was yet another incredible sight. From our MI-8's tiny window we saw the most incredible 'etched scene' of the mountains and the deep greens of some of the lakes, a very noisy ride but after just over an hour, we circled above our destination taking in the first glimpses of the most spectacular sight of all.

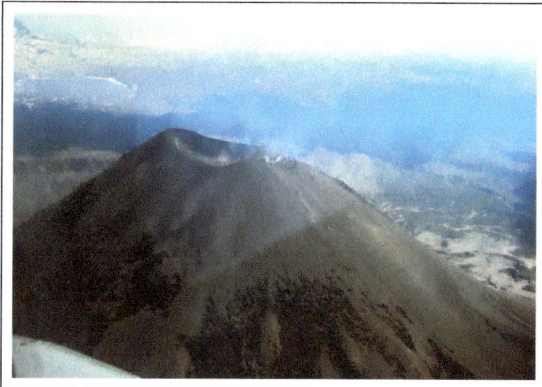

Known as 'The Valley of the Geyzers' it was only discovered in 1941 by Tatyana Ustinova and then sadly, more recently, in June 2007, much was devastated by a major landslide; we were able to hike and clamber up and down the wooden steps and boardwalks provided. These geysers are hot springs, warm pools and gurgling mud pots with a backdrop landscape 'painted' with

an amazing array of colours and textures from the minerals deposited in this geothermal wonderland. In this caldera alone there are over 1,000 hot springs of different sizes and forms. A bonus was the sight of brown bears, and spring flowers, brought on early by the geysers' warmth. We dragged ourselves back to the MI-8 for another noisy but thankfully safe journey back to the basic heliport outside Petropavlovsk.

The flight from London to Quito, Ecuador became a true adventure. We were doing well having refuelled at Bonaire and were getting on simply fine both amongst ourselves and also with our crew. The head stewardess was very chatty and before we landed at Guayaquil came with a large plastic bag telling us to not open it – but to enjoy it later. We didn't know that an announcement would follow explaining that we would not fly onto Quito but must disembark at Guayaquil where we would be given a flight on to Quito. The bag contained two bottles of champagne from 1st Class! The airport was in a state of complete mayhem with adults, children, pets and even caged birds all hustling. The saga we had gaining a journey to Quito is told elsewhere but in short it was a thorough nightmare, yet in the end most enjoyable. All the fun of travel!

Airports, whether in departure or at arrivals, are so diverse one could write a tome of experiences. Suffice it to say, we have seen endless examples, from the marble halls of Dubai, small canvas covers at game reserves to the most beautiful and unique Paro Airport, Bhutan. But when I arrived in New York, where one must collect one's own luggage before checking it in again, I found my alarm clock going off within my case. Panic. I have never travelled since without that same clock firmly closed having a rubber band around the switch!

Flying from Tanzania to Zanzibar my medical friend found that she did not have a yellow fever certificate, most necessary to take the flight. I gave her the list of injections that I had from my local practice, which when handed over was deemed 'all in order' – sometimes bullshit *is* required! Again having been to Tashi's passing out parade at NDA, he and I flew domestic from Bombay to Calcutta where we had to stay in the most awful airport accommodation overnight before flying into Bhutan; it was there at the Calcutta passport control Tashi realised that the Army had his passport not he. Oh my, there was no way I would leave him there on his own and no way can one leave a country, particularly India, without the correct paperwork, however by some incredible luck, a Bhutanese medical specialist was right

there watching the scenario and immediately became involved and somehow signed for Tashi and aboard we went. Phew!

After Tashi's three years at NDA he went on to IMA, near Dherham Dun. He invited me to his Pipping Ceremony and the honour of unveiling his Pips. I invited my nephew to travel with me for his 21st birthday present. We were away a very long weekend, each day travelling six to eight hours to our next point of call before finally making it to the Academy. I had booked our tickets the day I came out of hospital after knee surgery, and with only a few weeks before the event, I asked for a wheelchair, just in case. Birmingham Airport then offered a completely different journey when travelling to the plane in a wheelchair, most enlightening how many underground passages there are! Arriving at Delhi there was my chair waiting, again I was taken on a diverse route to the arrivals lounge to await our guide. I must admit that I was on the back of an elephant the next day! The whole trip was totally exhausting so when we arrived back at the airport and finally boarded, I was asleep before we even took to the air. My nephew nudged me as we taxied onto our Birmingham arrivals gate, I had slept the whole return journey!

Travelling within Guatemala from Guatemala City to Flores in the north our luggage was checked in group style, but the airport had made an error with my ticket thinking that Marie, my sister-in-law, and I were the same person and had simply deleted me. Our guides had to fight the good fight as the airport officials were just not going to accept that they had made the error. With phone calls to our company's secretary and faxed sheets of our tickets, they were still not budging. Meanwhile, I was

sitting quietly waiting, not in the slightest worried. First a lad came over to see if I would like a wheelchair – I didn't say that a ticket would be good – then another security gentleman came over; he was responsible for passengers flowing through the airport, I told him my problem, and off he went.

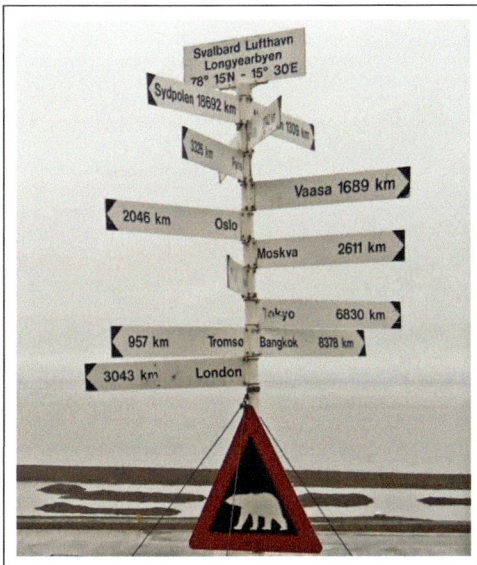

Finally, the airport manager came, produced a ticket, smiled, apologized and away we went.

We were advised that it was fine to purchase alcohol when stopping off to fuel at Bonaire, an island in the Leeward Antilles in the Caribbean Sea, on the way home from Guatemala. Infuriatingly, I found it being taken off me at Amsterdam Airport. I was livid and even after taking a firm stand accompanied by my friend, neither of us had any joy. One error I made was that I didn't break the bottle as it went into their 'booty' bin! But equally, when flying out of Heathrow for Norway and then onto Longyearbyen, Svalbard I was held for having a tiny sachet of silicon in my camera bag. After much pleading, I was allowed through with the security staff commenting 'mad woman', but not so when returning from Delhi to London with the same bag. There was something in there that the security just didn't like. We were very tight timewise for the flight, but still whatever it was couldn't be found, until finally my father's tiny mother of pearl penknife was discovered and therefore taken. I was so sad – it must have been there for about five years unused and undiscovered, virtually travelling the world.

My greatest bloomer was returning from Johannesburg to London after a month in the long-based Land Rover. We had tried to pack up the night before at our final campsite. Checking our tyres, we found our last one was worn down

to the wire mesh – best go steady was our comment, there was nothing else we could do! Leaving there the following morning we were heading down the wonderful tarmac road to Windhoek to deliver the vehicle – but exactly where to? I had no recollection of having had any instructions whatsoever – oh glory be! We continued, with me wracking my brain. I had our tennis club coach back home come into my mind: why on earth should I think of her at that very moment? Ah yes, her daughter worked for Wilderness Safaris, did they have an address in Windhoek? By chance I had one of their brochures, looked at the address and thought it best that we went there first.

Up we drove to a small cottage-style building and wonder of wonders, they were looking out for us, this was our destination. With a full year of planning, I certainly hadn't thought about that scenario. But, then onto the airport and a flight to Johannesburg. Happily checked in, luggage gone and with boarding cards in hand we were soon on our way. We landed with six hours to wait until our ongoing London flight. Once again, I was exhausted – but with mission accomplished as I thought, I promptly sat down and went to sleep while the other two wandered the shops and cafés.

Once the gate opened, we trundled down to board very pleased with ourselves – oh deary me, none of us had boarding cards and worse still, we hadn't collected our luggage and checked it onto this flight either! Advised that the flight was full, we were told to stand behind (memories of school!). I could hardly contain myself; this was shades of the airport programme where they film the most ridiculous things that ever must be faced! Amazingly, within minutes and numerous calls a most competent lady had boarding cards for us, even seated together which I felt was quite remarkable – where had they conjured those from considering it was a full flight and also, would our luggage be aboard? It was! Phew, that was a near thing after such a long and truly unique trip.

A friend of mine from home invited me out to her parent's farm in Bulawayo, then Rhodesia, for a trip. I enjoyed nearly three weeks in South Africa driving with another friend from Johannesburg down to the Garden route along to Durban and then back up to Johannesburg before flying to Bulawayo for a most interesting visit to that amazing country. There seemed to be excitement up front, but I didn't realise it was the Tribal Chief who was aboard, so as we disembarked there were thousands of tribesmen on the tarmac to greet him, waving, dancing and of course singing. That indeed was a wonderful way to arrive in Rhodesia.

In time, I was introduced to my friend's school pal Lynne who was very keen to go to Kenya and Tanzania to see the Great Migration. Twenty-two years went by before that was organised, she gathering five friends and me just one. The eight of us had a ball and have

59

travelled together many times since. Three bottled out when an elephant came rather close to them, causing much leg pulling from those of us in the other vehicle!

It was through dear Lynne that I came to make my epic Silver Gap trip when invited by one of these 'gals' to visit and travel with her in Queensland, New South Wales and Tasmania.

Arriving at Brisbane Airport from Singapore before flying onto Cairns my travelling chum and I were organising a local mobile phone. Once set up, we phoned our friend who answered immediately and gave me the sad news that Lynne, who, as I have said, had instigated our friendship and trip, had died at exactly the moment we had landed in my 7th continent, Australia. Happily, I had spoken to Lynne before leaving home and was able to say goodbye including as always plenty of laughs. Since then we have all continued to travel, meeting up at the most unlikely airports but always with memories of our dear Lynne.

Celia had spent a full year putting together our trip across South America in 1980. On arrival at my house she advised me that our flight from Miami to Buenos Aires had been cancelled by L.A.B. and there was nothing that the travel agent could do about it. So, on arrival at Miami we endured six hours of stress as there was no one at the Bolivian Airways counter at all. We kept using our quarters to phone the office in town, who said they would be with us within the hour. This happened many times but they were simply a 'no show'. In the end we secured a flight with Air Chile, but only if we could get our present ticket stamped and signed. Luckily the Bolivian Airways counter was beside Air Chile so being rather bold I went into the abandoned office and found the necessary rubber stamp, initialled it myself and presented the tickets. Oh my, were we glad to be in the air that time! Being on a slightly earlier flight we arrived in Buenos Aires sooner than expected and were able to connect to a better flight to Montevideo, our final destination that day.

Looking down on my favourite airport, Paro, Bhutan I could see the challenge of landing onto a very short runway between very steep mountains. Only the national airline Druk Air, Royal Bhutan Airlines, is allowed to land there which is most gratifying considering one passes the roofs of the local houses with many drying chillies before finally touching down. From here Sonam, Tashi's wife, and I set off on our way to the family farmhouse a little further up the valley.

787:4200:113:563 :2

Passenger Ticket and Baggage Check

DRUK AIR

Royal Bhutan Airlines

Issued by **DRUK AIR CORPORATION LTD.** Thimphu, Bhutan

Those were days when airlines required a ticket; this was my ticket back in 1998.

From that airport on Jersey to the ultra-modern Dubai Airport, multi-paged tickets to the simple method of scanning one's passport, airport travel has moved on but so too has the length of the hiking required to reach either the gate or baggage reclaim; travel is most certainly by far a more complicated passage via today's airports.

Chapter 6
Cooking and Catering

Travelling on an organised trip along the Carrao River beneath the Angel Falls, the World's highest waterfall, Venezuela, we were required to assist with the cooking in the evenings. Having struggled off the river, decanted all the equipment from our two bongos, hung our hammocks beneath a simple palm roof but still beside the 'beach' it was then all hands to the pump to help prepare our dinner. Chickens from our floating pantry for our first evening travelled plucked but not drawn – apparently to retain their freshness; these had to be dealt with and then put onto wigwam-style stakes, having been immersed in adobo flavouring. This BBQ beside the river deep in the jungle was simply incredible. Water was heated in a witch-like black cauldron over the fire. To make coffee, the grounds were spooned in, brought up to just below the boil when an eggshell was added which sent the grounds to the bottom – we were all on a steep learning curve!

The Waterfall is 979 metres high and was discovered by James Angel in 1933, becoming a UNESCO World Heritage Site in 1944. Tourism was opened in 1990, *just* a short while before our 1993 trip. It 'enjoys' the highest humidity in the World, raining every day except between December and March!

The local fauna surrounding our shelter

included jaguars, monkeys, giant ant eaters, iguanas, parrots, fulmars and macaws to mention a few, besides over 300 species of plants including many endemics. I have failed to mention the giant ants, especially those who 'feasted on me'! I was happily enclosed in my cotton sleeping sheet within the hammock, the humidity not requiring me to use my sleeping bag until about 4am; but when gathering it up from beneath, little did I realise that the itching I soon succumbed to was provided by those critters who had hitched a lift into my hammock. The wheals, the squashed blighters and the blood were all there in technicolour come dawn, their form of jungle-catering – but, the view from my hammock was spectacular!

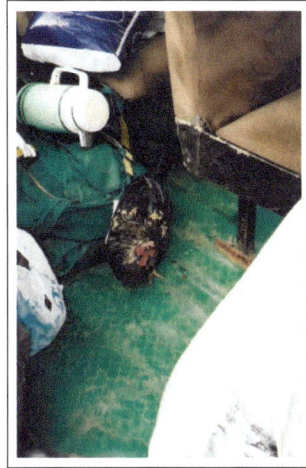

Leaving Addis Ababa, Ethiopia for Debark, we collected our cook and a guard for one night up in the Simeon Mountains. Once we had finally gathered up our 'chef' he then had to do his shopping which included a chicken who sat just by Rob's feet in our van plus enough spices for the rest of our trip! As we climbed, the terrain became ever rougher, and the round houses were now stone based. Ancient hedera and hypericum trees were everywhere, lots of wildflowers, alpines and finally troupes of Gelada baboons, some small but others enormous. I was out and amongst one troupe that must have amounted to at least 400 of these spectacular creatures. A true experience.

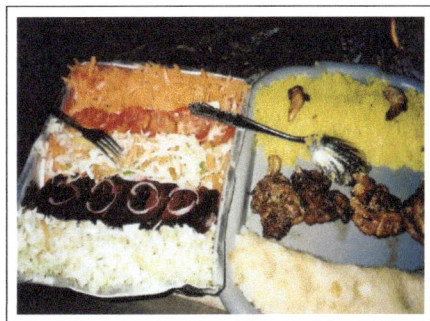

Rob simply sat there with his chicken watching him, but once up at the summit where our tents were put up for us, the chicken was very soon destined for the pot and onto our plates! Stephen had a conscience over the future of our travelling companion and decided that the whisky bottle was the best remedy. Rob and I were just looking forward to a darn good meal! However, many whiskies and a very good meal later we

63

were escorted by our armed guard to our tents: Stephen's was a single long tube affair soon named 'wasps-nest' plus an unprintable prefix! Although I always wear earplugs in these situations, I did hear a commotion but thought nothing of it. Poor Stephen was trying to get out of his nest for a wee and was having a great deal of trouble – the language was apparently more than amusing! That was a very cold night with an extremely hard frost. I didn't need to get dressed; I had only taken off my boots!

Camping trips have been fun, one never knows where one's tent has been put up, is it on the flat? Not always, it certainly wasn't in Rwanda. Is the ground lumpy? Often, even on the beach in Oman. How quiet is the area? Who are the likely visitors – dogs, predators, birdlife, reptiles, insects? Camping in Bhutan was excitingly unpredictable especially when visited by the locals who were the gentlest and kindest people ever. I looked out for tigers, snow leopards and the Yeti known there as 'Migoi' (strong man) or 'Gredpo'. Yes, we did find the fresh footprints of a snow leopard when going 'bushy-bushy' across the snow and had sightings of red panda, golden langurs and various monkeys, many yaks and the

ever-visiting wild boar. The cooking was done for us in Bhutan, and we just had to be able to cope with the enormous number of chillies that went into virtually every dish. On average, they will eat 10 each day!

Right out in the middle of the mountains we would stop beside the road for our lunch. Time mattered not, our position was based on the view which was always fabulous or beside a spectacular chorten. Our

picnic was served hot out of stacked thermo containers, all so very well organised. Nearly always, wherever one is in the world, it is a remarkable thing that children appear from 'nowhere'. Dependent on the country the aroma

they bring is diverse, but their smiles and friendship are always enormous.

It was a monk who was our saviour one afternoon when climbing the mountain behind Thimpu, capitol of Bhutan, while on a trek to see the meconopsis (Bhutan's national flower). We were stranded in Bhutan for three days as our departure plane was out of order giving us time to enjoy this extra adventure. Along with our Bhutanese guide, we had our cook and the horseman with his beasts carrying all our requirements. Within an hour of setting off the rain started to fall and continued to increase as the afternoon went on. Finding a suitable flat area to put up the tents our assistant soon found water rushing off the mountain straight through our 'camp'. By the time we made this height, camping, yes I am slow uphill, was almost abandoned but what to do? We found a wooden shed nearby as well as some sticks, so lit a fire to try to keep warm. Tashi, our guide very wisely went to the nearby monastery to ask if there was any way we could stay there overnight. He returned with a very relieved smile upon his face as one of the monks had offered us his

room as well as another room where our cook and horseman could stay. Safe within the confines of this relatively small monastery high up on the mountain we began to dry out beside the wood burning stove in the centre of this monastic cell while the rain continued outside.

Of course we had all our own equipment so were totally self-accommodating. After our dinner our kindly monk left us to camp down on the wooden floor using our sleeping bags – yes that was a hard surface! But more amusing was the worry I had regarding all the

holiday money that had become totally soaked within my bum bag. I laid it all around the burner hoping that by morning the notes would have dried out;

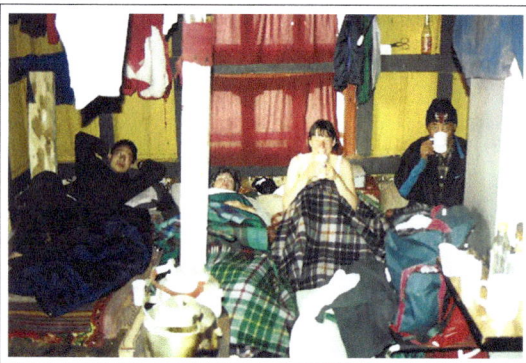

but oh no, within minutes of 'torches out' there were scratching sounds running around above us. Glory be, it was the monk's resident rats – oh no, were they after my dollar bills?! Each time they were on the run I switched on my torch for them to scuttle off but finally, I had to gather up the money abandoning that form of saving them. The morning brought sunshine upon the mountainside which was lucky as the need for a nature call was much required but with no facilities it was a bushy-bushy visit yet again!

Our cook was setting up breakfast outside which was simply incredible, even though the ground was so wet. He gave us a camping table and chairs, but the view will stay with me forever, there was a thick blanket of cloud below us, almost as if we were in a plane looking down, with a perfect blue sky above. Needless to say, we returned back down the mountain without ever reaching the famous area of those glorious blue poppies and leaving our kindly monk with his rodent friends.

My biggest challenge regarding catering was when I hired a long-wheelbase Land-Rover to travel for a month through Botswana and Namibia. Before leaving I had my fellow travellers lined up; a cousin who would share the driving, help put the roof camp beds up and down plus do the washing up and

another friend who would keep the vehicle clean and tidy. We had a guide for the Botswanan Safari section, who would drive within the Okavango

and of course do the most important job, the spotting, leaving me to do the balance of the driving and all the cooking and catering. Once out of the Delta our guide left us, but I had another friend who lived in Gaborone who joined us to enjoy the Kalahari salt pans and after that a farmer friend from home who would be on Braai duty, vehicle maintenance, some driving and most importantly, be on gin-and-tonics duty for the Namibian leg!

Like so many trips the logistics are enormous. It took me a full year to put together where we could shop, gain fuel and water, find campsites and most importantly, discover the mileage and conditions between. I took notes from various guidebooks for all the sights and places of interest that we shouldn't miss, plus noting that there were not many shops to be found, few garages, but many, many miles of graded and non-graded roads.

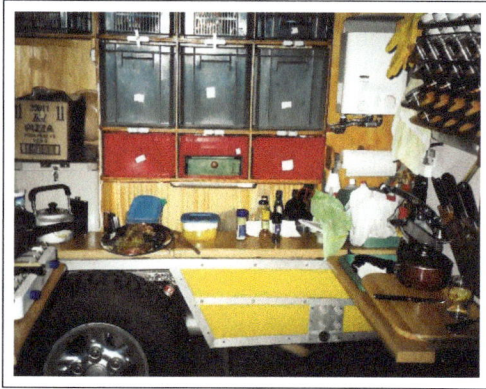

A shopping list was forwarded to our guide's girl friend who kindly purchased as much as was available for our arrival. I took out lots of packets of custard to simply add water, dried fruit to be rehydrated, packets of cappuccino, porridge oats and various kitchen tools.

The vehicle was fabulous and extremely compact, converted by a boat builder. Getting everything stashed away was a big job, especially as we arrived to terrific heat and had only a short time before departing.

At our first picnic stop we lost our loaf of bread to a monkey, who was well pleased with himself. The eggs had also come to grief but after that life simply became a pleasant challenge. We had amazing meals conjured out of 'not a lot', always porridge for breakfast with long life milk. Mid sunrise safari coffee was easily provided, sometimes with cake or a biscuit but after our first encounter, there was always a sharp eye for that evil monkey's relative, a hyena or even those blessed critters – the ants!

The gas lasted out; the water was easily gained but would our initial pantry last until our return to Maun? Our trip to the salt pans provided the cook two nights off before returning to Maun to say goodbye to one friend and meet another; this was also my 2nd shopping opportunity. While in

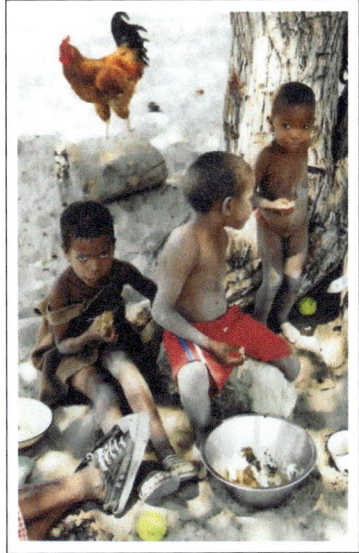

the Kalahari we were invited to breakfast with a Kalahari bushman family; they were simply delightful and most welcoming offering us fried mopani worms amongst other delicacies – most certainly a change from the daily porridge!

With store cupboards and freezer restored to health, we left Maun and were away off to Namibia. First, we had to get through border control but not before hiding the forbidden fresh and frozen meat; *phew*: no one checked – maybe the friendly 'good morning, what a glorious day' provoked the officer into waving us straight through! We managed for a long time before our next chance when reaching the Skeleton Coast; but for a famous butcher in the middle of nowhere, that was our only shopping. Fuel was purchased at every opportunity; we were not going to find ourselves without.

However, wheel changing duties coincided with my cooking, we laughed each time as the vehicle appeared to be slipping forward, lacking an effective brake – one just can't get the staff!

When wanting to get a better position to watch both a lion sheltering under a bush and a rhino on the other side, the vehicle failed to start. So there we were, unable to get out, unable to start the engine, no one around at all and the temperature mighty high. We tried everything we could but to no avail. Finally, a car came along with an English family aboard and although they had never towed a vehicle, let alone a well-loaded large, long-wheelbase Land Rover, they were happy to assist. With eyes firmly on both lion and rhino I was up on the roof gathering our camp bed straps; they were fitted beneath the front of our vehicle and onto the rear of our saviours' car. With instructions to not use the brake we were pulled remarkably well all 20 odd miles straight into camp and to our site. Cousin Jude went in search of someone who knew about Land Rovers, happily finding one immediately, who came once he had enjoyed his lunch, and we ours: catering must continue! Thankfully he was successful in a very short time. The battery connection had come apart; fixed, we were happy campers again. However, at the beginning of our evening safari I was driving and having gone out of the camp gates I thought I should just test the starter. Switched off but again, the engine failed to start. Out I jumped, lifted the passenger seat to reach the battery to jam it back together – which was when the guards came thundering down on me – my, where were they that morning when we really were in dire straits? All part of great trips!

Heading back towards Windhoek and the end of our trip, we stayed at our last safari park at the Waterberg Plateau, where we were given a great camping site beneath the breathtaking, high red sandstone escarpment. We gathered up a young German couple walking down the road who were apparently camping quite near us, they appeared to be the only other folk at the site. We invited them to join us for drinks and then dinner, especially as they had discovered that their tent had been vandalized by baboons. We all enjoyed each other's company, a very boozy evening and somehow, I managed to conjure up a five-course meal for the six of us on two small rings and a braai!

On our final evening, dinner was a combination of leftovers, but I still had eggs and bread and thought it a good idea to make egg sandwiches for our wonderful driver, mechanic and pre-prandial provider's journey. These he took, popping them into the top of his bag. Bless him, his luggage failed to meet him in Johannesburg, it was finally delivered to his house in England a whole week later by which time he was busy back out on the farm. Another week went by before time was found to unpack. Oh dear two-week-old egg sandwiches are not good amongst one's clothes – another travel lesson!

Travel plans occasionally have an amazing twist of fortune, sometimes for the worse, sometimes the better. We planned a trip to KwaZulu-Natal one January, flying to Durban where we hired what we thought was a 4x4, only to discover when

we became stuck that it was only a 2x4. The Rhino Charity gained when we paid to be pulled out. However, after a full week at the Tembe Game Reserve, where we were catered for fantastically, we wished to stay at Phinda Reserve, but could anyone get in touch with them to book us in – non? We decided that we would just drive there and hopefully be able to stay, self-catering or not. We couldn't find the reserve even given maps, GPS and instructions; so, having failed miserably we drove onto Hluhluwe-Umfolozi Game Reserve which we knew well.

The previous evening there had been a single lady sitting at the manager's dinner table. We hadn't seen her before and commented that she must be on business. We thought no more until leaving the following morning on our quest to find Phinda and after having to alter our plan, we reached the entrance gate to Hluhluwe.

Leaving my cousin at the wheel, I met a lady in the gatehouse office doorway who asked if I could split a note for her, because she needed change. I told her to go to the vehicle right there at the barrier where Jude had our kitty. Thinking no more, I entered and requested a self-catering Rondavel for two nights, whereupon I was given a very firm no, unless I had proof of a booking. I would have to drive back 30 miles across the pot-holed road to the Hluhluwe Village to find accommodation. Horrified, I said certainly not. The gate officer's argument was the shortage of water. While arguing the toss, the lady returned to the counter and, upon hearing my disquiet, intervened. She wished to help and suggested that we could share the oversized Rondavel that she was booked into; I warmed to her and said thank you, even without discussing it with Jude – she seemed such a genuine person. Our officer continued to be extremely negative, but she was not one to be beaten. She was onto the main camp office straight away to ask if she could add two extra people to her booking: no problem. There was much huffing and puffing, double scanning of our passports and paperwork before our disgruntled member of staff finally raised the barrier! Back in our vehicle Jude questioned whether this lady was the same person who had been at dinner the previous evening? On arrival at the main camp, we asked her and yes indeed, it was. How amazing is that, what are the odds of meeting at a doorway, when one was planning to be elsewhere?

At the desk there was absolutely no problem, we were even able to have our own Rondavel, therefore not having to share. Jude and I planned to go on the evening organised safari and then dine in the restaurant so invited our new friend to join us. What a joy, she was the most incredible person, travelling Africa alone in her hired truck. She could spot any animal or bird, name them as well as knowing their sex and age. We spent the next two days with her totally animated by her knowledge and stories.

I believe the moral to this is that self-catering is just wonderful, but when being catered for, do take into account the other clients. You never know where they will turn up as they are doing just what you are doing. On other trips this has happened several times, most certainly when hiring unique vehicles. People have stopped us at garages to have a closer look having seen us at campsites or out on the road. Always such fun.

The camaraderie at many of the camp sites we have visited has been terrific and often as enlightening as the area and experiences available. On our tour around both North and South Islands, New Zealand in 2013 we arrived at Twizel, near Lakes Pukaki and Tekapo, where we found the managers most delightful and able to answer many of our questions. They had only one unpowered site left, so we accepted and paid immediately. When they took us there, they realised that there was a powered site they had forgotten about, so very generously it was ours with no extra charge. A bonus also was that our neighbours and their visitors invited us to join them after dinner. We enjoyed a most friendly round of enthusiasm, advice and fun. They were all fishermen and had caught far too many and were determined that we should fill our fridge with their overflow – we accepted! Lake Twizel has an enormous quantity of trout in it, it is free to fish but no one can sell the fish.

On this same trip we had been unable to find the place to put the pipe for the grey water. We had been searching underneath, all around the outside, to no avail, time and time again. Parked beside a Japanese family with an enormous Winnebago-style vehicle, he was our man, he went straight to it – it was behind the open sliding door! We had obviously never looked when the door was closed; that had only taken us just short of three weeks to find!

During our final camp on our return to Brisbane we came a cropper as far as finding a campsite that was not fully booked. It was interesting too, as the previous night we couldn't book ahead, whereas here we should have! When Jude went into the reception the lady was hoping that we had a booking, but she did advise where we might find a good 'freedom camp' – which turned out to be the one I had mentally noted as we came along the Indian Ocean Highway. We sped back rapidly and yes;

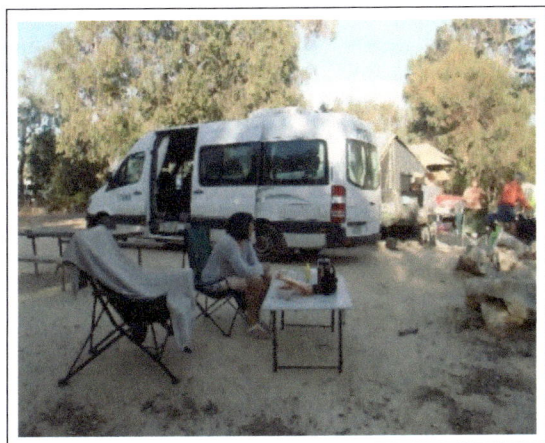

indeed, it was the self-same one with good facilities and even a dump. We were able to pull right up beside the Moore River and farmland with lots of birds flitting in and out, perfect.

Gradually, the whole area was rapidly filling up, starting with a lovely family right next to us. They came with an incredible tent/trailer system which went up in minutes, and in turn were joined by further family with ever more amazing equipment. This whole family were certainly camping professionals! The three sisters, mothers of the various tribes, had emigrated from Malvern back in the 50s on the £10 scheme. Amusingly, with just one night in Brisbane before we (the amateurs) were due to hand our trusty campervan back, we discovered that the passenger seat also swung around to the central dining table – it had only taken us 20 days! We will know for next time …

However, having camped in the Selous Game Park, Tanzania I meandered into the 'kitchen' interested to see how the cook had been able to conjure up our meals: I could but only take this image. Suffice it to say, we have all survived the experience, but I was pleased that I hadn't visited on the first day! Happy travelling.

Chapter 7
Storms

We have all been caught in a storm, be it in our local high street having just popped around the corner for a loaf of bread or down on the beach on what appeared to be a gloriously peaceful sunny day. If you are on the beach and a squall or torrential rain suddenly comes along, sand gets in every crevice and all your paraphernalia goes everywhere – then suddenly, as quick as it started, it stops and calm follows.

Travelling around the world is no different, but one tends to remember the greater moments with a smile or even an enormous laugh at the predicament in which one finds oneself.

One of our sudden, (in this case very sudden) decisions was to sail to Stewart Island off the south coast of South Island, New Zealand. Ten minutes to park our campervan, pack our bag and be on the catamaran with certainly no time for a sea-sickness pill, even if I had thought about it! Most exciting, we knew little of what was on the island other than the rare endemic birds; we had no accommodation or knowledge of what was available. The journey was about an hour, easy peasy I thought, she who is poorly on a lilo in a swimming pool. The captain did say the ocean was lumpy, he was right! The waves were enormous, thankfully he rode them well. Oh yes, so did I for the first 35 minutes but after that, the fact that the waters are notably the 3rd roughest in the world really hit hard. Dear me, but so prepared are they that they have a nurse at hand to deal with 'us all'! She was gallantly waiting there ready with ice-cold towels not only for hands but more importantly for wrapping around the back of the neck. A miracle – oh my, I couldn't recommend the method more highly.

Sadly, neither the crew, fellow passengers nor I knew this remedy when we sailed from Miavaig Quay, Uig, Lewis towards St Kilda – the furthest west of the Scottish Outer Hebridean Islands. With just a light swell for about two hours we entered Loch Tamnavray, a small sea inlet southwest of Harris enjoying wonderful sightings. We anchored offshore overnight and come morning we discovered it to be simply the best breakfasting spot. White-tailed eagles flew overhead, together with sightings of herons, peregrine falcons, seals, fulmars, gannets, cormorants, shags and skuas, as we continued off Scarp heading west into the Atlantic across the sea to our destination.

Once out of the shelter of the loch the sea soon sorted me out and forced me to leave the deck and take to the dining table's bench seat: prostrate, I dared not go below! The voyage on these high seas took six hours, and I hasten to add that I wasn't the only one to suffer. Happily, I was forced back out on deck to enjoy the marvels of nature in the form of sheer cliffs rising hundreds of feet from the sea to rock crags covered with thousands of nesting and attendant seabirds.

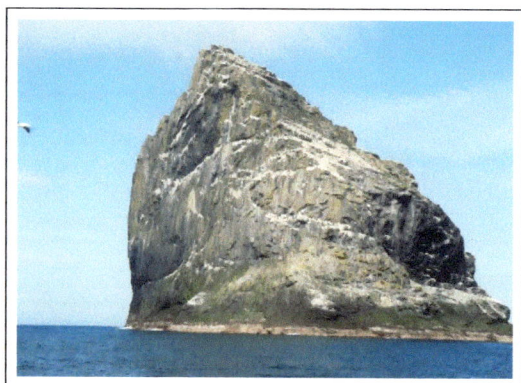

The sound of all those birds was truly moving as we sailed around the Stacs: Boreray, Lee and an Armin; I have to say I felt 'oceans' better and am ever thankful to my fellow sailors for not allowing me to miss such a fabulous sight.

While we are over there at the western limits of Great Britain, I must tell the tale of the most extraordinary coincidence. My friends always tell me that I can't go anywhere without meeting someone I know or friends of friends. Having anchored off Village Bay, our skipper said that he felt it a good idea to go ashore, meet the National Trust manager and learn the geography before spending the following full day ashore. So, at about 4.30pm we clambered down the rope ladder into the dinghy, about three at a time, to be taken to the concrete steps which is the St Kilda Quay. Fine, I was complete with day sack containing cameras and now enjoying a far better 'tummy' state.

It being low tide, we arrived at the base of quite a few steps onto which I threw my bag before clambering almost on all fours safely out onto the quay. When finally upright, I was facing a gentleman who I had met on a cruise out of Vancouver. He and his lady friend were standing there watching this whole performance with amusement but all I could think to say was "Good Lord, last seen up the Inside Passage" – the look on the lady's face will remain in my memory for ever. Shock horror! However, we had a darn good laugh and natter which is what life is all about. I believe we have both used that story at many a dinner party!

I smile when I think of the insufficient weather gear that I took on that Inside Passage voyage. I had no idea that I was going into an area of extremely high rainfall. Our cabin was continuously akin to a Chinese laundry until we came into the Wrangell Narrows and finally the village of Petersburg, home of the largest home-based halibut fleet in Alaska; just the right place to boast a shop selling the real gear. Happily choosing to go on a wildflower guided walk we were out on the bog when down came ever more precipitation, this time in a big way, soaking us once again. We were heading back into the village looking like drowned rats, still enjoying the lush gardens, when a lady whose planting design we were just discussing, drove up to her house and started chatting. We asked which would be the best place to purchase satisfactory kit; not only did she advise but invited us into her vehicle and took us straight there introducing us to the proprietor. She told us that they all have three sets of gear: one off, one on and one still drying. I walked out of the shop dressed in my new purchases with my wet clothes in the shop carrier bag!

The Napo River, a great tributary to the almighty Amazon was yet another occasion when the storm hit. We had gone out for a 36-hour sortie onto the river, its tributaries and lakes and planned to sleep overnight beside a salt lick in hope of sighting jaguar and other nocturnal creatures.

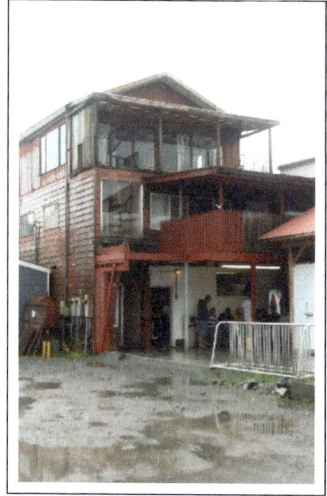

Leaving the Secret Lake and coming back onto the Napo River watching a pod of freshwater dolphins (those glorious pink ones) the heavens opened

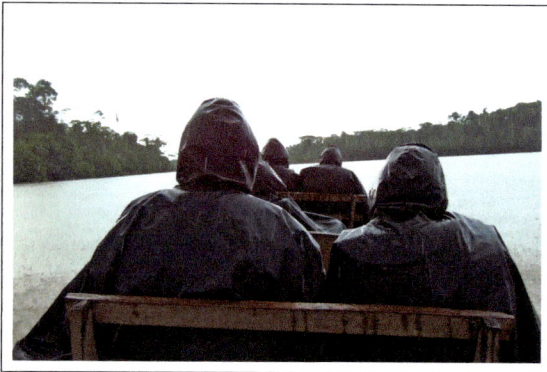

and oh my, I have never suffered such driving hail like it. Even with full length ponchos we were being battered as if by nails. The rain continued for 12 hours raising this almighty river by some four feet. Our wonderful boatman stripped off

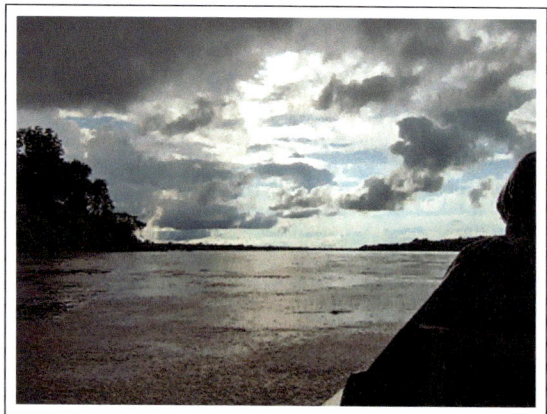

naked (out of our sight) and took all our bedding to the lick after which we trundled through the jungle to take up our night stop.

Our sleeping at the salt lick was interesting but what sane animal would be out in that weather?

None! One must just put these escapades down to experience and continue to laugh. We have done so, many a time.

A similar storm hit in Botswana when out on the most glorious (as we thought) afternoon Mokoro Safari. Sitting back in one of the traditional wooden canoes that are so famed within the Okavango was simply heaven, gliding through the papyrus, with sitatunga, elephants, kingfishers, herons, waterbuck and hippos around us when slowly the sky changed, the blue became darker and darker reaching the colour of our old school ink. Suddenly the birds went silent and then the powers from above let rip with enormous cracks of thunder, the sky was lit by great streaks of lightning and finally the rain, hail and wind erupted. Oh my, I have never seen such a wonderful storm, the fact that I was continuously bailing out and trying to stop the hail from grating my face was by the by, the experience was 'Just Africa' at its greatest. Pure nature.

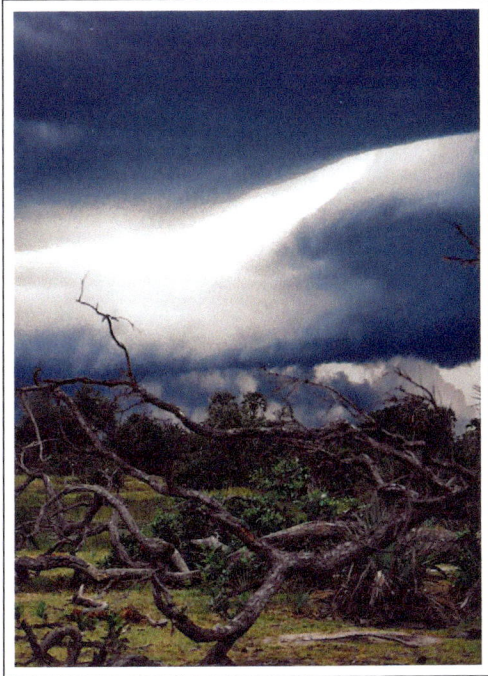

Returning home from Virginia Beach, beside Chesapeake Bay, USA. I was on a Norfolk, Virginia flight to Washington. For some reason I was in row one which faced down the plane towards the back. Fine by me, that was a different experience. The plane was flying at capacity, with 90% service personnel from the naval and air force bases. We had almost arrived at Washington when a lightning storm hit, oh my. I have never seen or experienced anything like it aboard; each time the plane dropped I could see every single passenger leave their seat and then fall back into place. There were three pilots working full time to keep the plane airborne. None of the staff were able to care for the ashen and soon very poorly passengers. It was horrendous but one could do nothing but just hang on in and pray. Talk about having a seat in the front stalls, I had a view in technicolour on that flight! In the end having flown over the Washington River we were not allowed to land and were required to return to Norfolk. The sight of so many of those passengers was not good; many, although offered a flight the next morning said that they would never fly again – airmen, marines, businessmen and sailors alike! Taxis were rapidly sought to take those who really needed to be in Washington. For my part, I rang my friend, who had already stripped my bed, to say that I was sorry, she hadn't got rid of me yet! I braved and thankfully enjoyed a calm flight the next day.

Returning on my first adventure to the Antarctic we knew that the Drakes Passage could be a challenge, most certainly when one of the engineers came to our cabin to lock the indoor porthole, we knew we were in for the 'Drake Shake', oh boy, did we get it too. I took

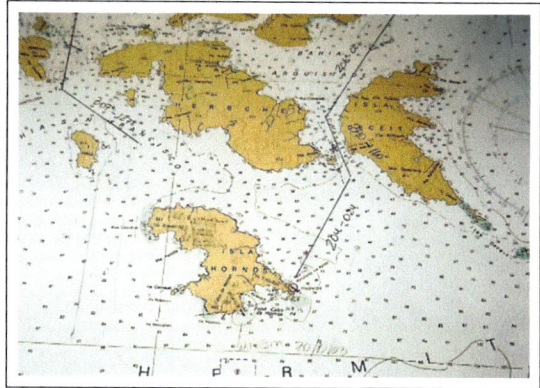

to my bed immediately. I knew I would be best there, for the St Kilda trip had taught me a lesson, but I didn't realise how much I would have to hang on to stay in place! Survive we did …

There were many fantastic skies down in Antarctica but one that blew my mind was the sheer beauty of the lenticular clouds that came over our boat one evening after dinner. I learned that these clouds form mostly in the troposphere generally in parallel alignment to the wind direction.

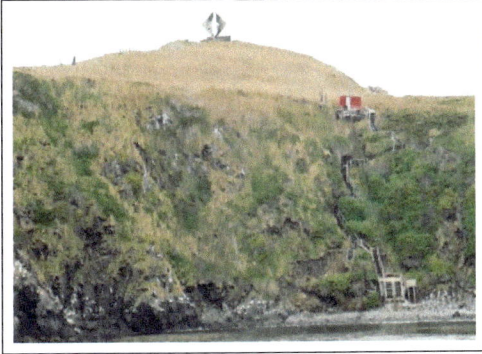

Cape Horn has happily been amazingly kind to me. Our first trip down there was when we sailed the Beagle Channel with the intention of landing at Cape Horn if conditions allowed it. My geography lessons had never enlightened me that Cape Horn is an island, that was a revelation.

Yes, we landed, walked up the steps and along the board walk to the top – incredible. Once back aboard our captain announced that as it was so calm, we would sail right around the island. Wow.

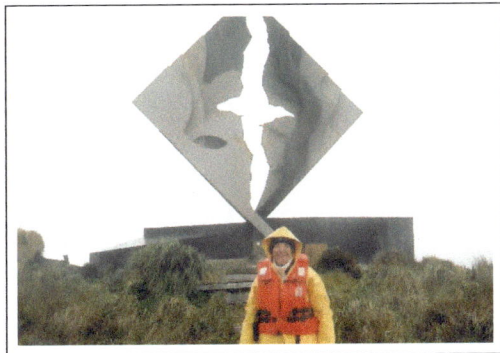

Returning once again across the Drakes Passage on our Shackleton Centenary voyage the waters were as calm as could possibly be. Any visions of the hundreds of sailing ships being lost in those waters seemed imaginary. We arrived off the Horn hours before our pilot was due

to meet us to sail back up the Beagle Channel, so most of us were out on deck enjoying our pre-prandial while watching the most beautiful rainbow out to sea with numbers of mighty albatross flying by. Nature at its very best, but as always, we must be ready to take the rough with the smooth and always with a smile and much appreciation.

Chapter 8
Markets

The daughter of a farmer and corn merchant, I was brought up well versed in deals. I listened to my father offering figures for haystacks, bales of straw, tons of wheat, oats or barley from a specific field or granary. Going to the cattle market to buy and sell farm animals or simply walking through the Thursday street market in Banbury during my school lunch hour, I suppose haggling and knowing the figure one is happy with became my 'DNA'! I therefore love the hustle and bustle of street and rural markets along with the camaraderie, fun and surprises when travelling in so many countries. The colour is always dramatic, the determination of the locals to either completely ignore the obvious tourist or to warmly welcome and be ready for fun. The variety of markets is diverse and the aroma from these fun destinations sometimes extremely challenging!

Addis Ababa market, reputably the largest in Africa, turned out to be the 'ripest' of any once we neared the butchery section. The whole area, in grid form, was open to the sun with stall holders providing their own cover if afforded. Gullies criss-crossed the area which was really no more than an open sewer, but for all that, everyone was so cheerful, ready to speak as best we could converse, or gesticulate and sell if possible. I loved the diversity of that market, but my companions couldn't hack it for long so sadly we did have to leave.

The much smaller old Stone Market in Zanzibar was very similar, but it was the first time that I had been extremely saddened by the modern culture of plastic and batteries being simply thrown out. The cows were wandering over the rubbish

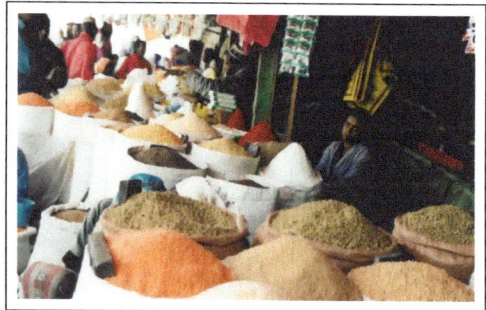

heaps which were filled with endless blue plastic bags, – it was a wonder their milk wasn't coloured. Quantities of batteries of all sizes in the ditches,

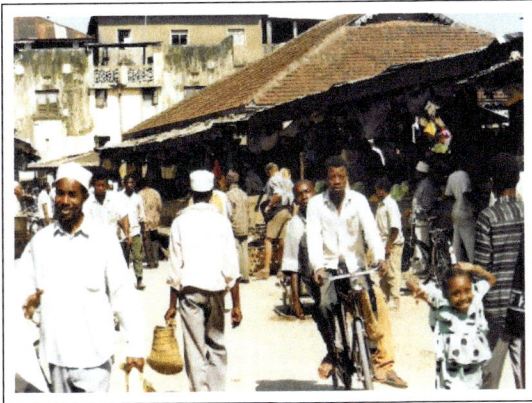

gullies and curbs left me very disturbed.

Cuzco's covered market back on All Saints Day 1980 was a revelation. We had trundled down the high street market stalls with their wares displayed at the side of the path including foetuses of llama for planting to satisfy Mama Pacha, who would then provide, they believed, a good crop. When we entered the great doors, we found an amazingly noisy indoor market with many proud Peruvian ladies sitting on high stools behind their various stalls and counters calling for custom and shouting their prices. It was

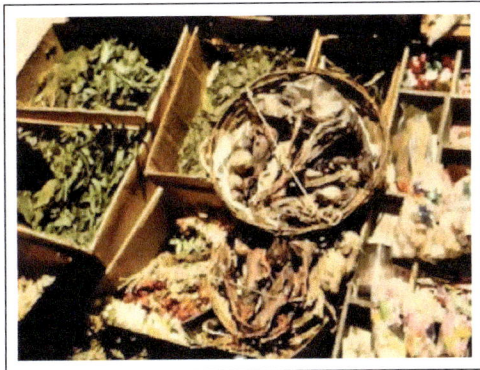

organised chaos and so much fun. The tradition for this feast day is T'anta wawa (baby bread); a sweet bread made in the shape of a baby and decorated with a plaster or bread face and wearing

a cap. The shape is that of a baby walteado, meaning wrapped in a blanket, so that only the face is visible. All ages were leaving with arms laden with these and other commodities, which we watched in wonderment. Sadly, Cusco was rife with thieves and needless to say the tourist was their prime target. On that trip we always carried our paper money between two socks within lace-up shoes, but this didn't stop a pair of children aged about six trying to knock

83

me off my balance intending to relieve me of whatever was in my pocket. Unhappily for them, they failed but I did feel sorry that they were driven to such practices at that tender age.

The poverty of Malawi was obvious as soon as we left Lilongwe to travel by road to Blantyre. Little children standing on the side of the road slowed us down to offer tiny crustaceans they had caught in the river, neatly packaged in hand-woven reed purses. We were offered cooked mice, a tiny live mouse lemur as well as fruit, vegetables and even rocks. Bless.

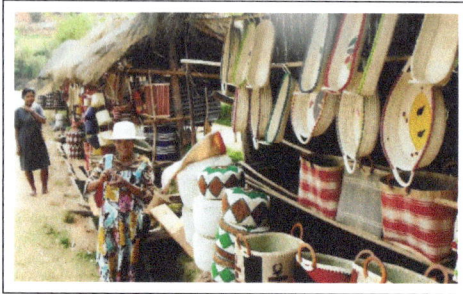

Madagascar was completely different as the districts we travelled through appeared to have highly individual crafts. Our guide did warn us that if we saw what we liked we should buy right then, such helpful advice. One area would sell floppy hats and baskets, another woodwork, then there were the districts for gems, pottery, carved ecclesiastical wooden statues, carved or even etched bone work made from their Zebu cattle horn. We visited an island where the ladies specialised in embroidery

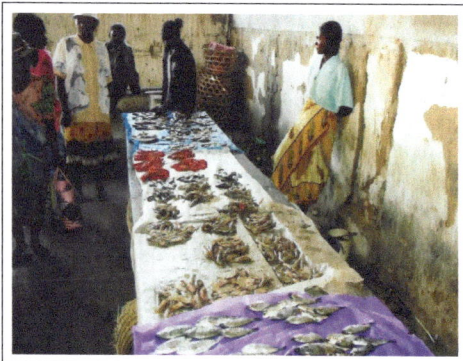

and drawn threadwork as well as tie and dye silk; these were incredible to find down on the beach beside the fishermen and their basic boats.

Every village seemed to have a marketplace too; chickens for sale from baskets lined up along the path, spices and herbs in rolled down cotton sacks; meat, fish and vegetables all laid out artistically – certainly nothing wasted and little of it plastic.

Both Ethiopia and Oman offered me the sight of camel markets, an incredible experience. My guidebook had mentioned one in Ethiopia, so when we happened to stay overnight in Negele I asked specifically if we could visit the enclosed market area before leaving town. Our guide was non-plussed, he knew nothing of it, but agreed. We found an area about the size of a rugby pitch with tiny, apparently static, huts down one side where the cameleer families had camped overnight. The centre was filled with camels of all kinds, differing in age, colour and nature. Some were spitting, others snarling, some sitting down, others kicking – it was a free for all and certainly

a dangerous place. There was much haggling going on, bartering and shouting, and finally the clap of hands and money being exchanged. Meanwhile, goats were being hung by a sack placed beneath their belly on spring scales – these

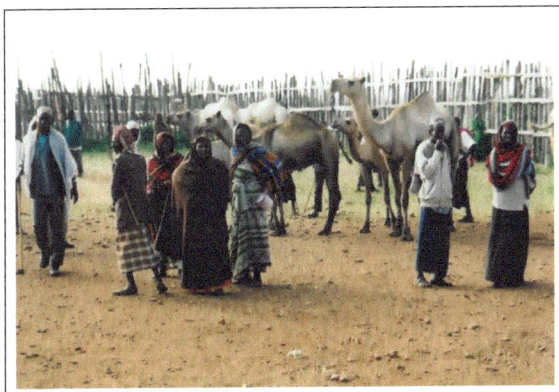

were obviously sold by weight. What an experience, which happily we came away from free of biting insects, kicks and spit!

Travelling from Al Ain to Oman we stopped off at a much smaller affair near the border, again with a variety of camels, all hobbled; some handsome (if that is possible of a camel), some large, others with calf but all of diverse shades. We did have to laugh at the giant size bras that the camel mothers were wearing to prevent their young from taking the milk but this time we didn't escape scot-free: my friend, our host, was kicked badly right on the knee by a mother who lashed back with her rear leg. Ouch. However, we were given a large bottle of camel's milk to enjoy with our lunch. Delicious.

The night before, we had gone out into the dunes taking a BBQ and chairs and sat back to watch the setting sun as the racing camels were put through their paces along the sandy route, tiny jockeys firmly aloft while the trainers and owners drove along in enormous 4x4s. It was surreal!

Simple basic fish sales straight from the boat had been interesting as there are generally more pelicans or storks queueing than customers, in Ethiopia on the shores of Lake Awassa where a simple boat came in from the lake with the overnight catch to be greeted by three tourists, one customer and a great quantity of birds.

And in Uganda, on the shores of Lake Victoria, we visited a village just as the men were coming ashore; it was mayhem as the children were more

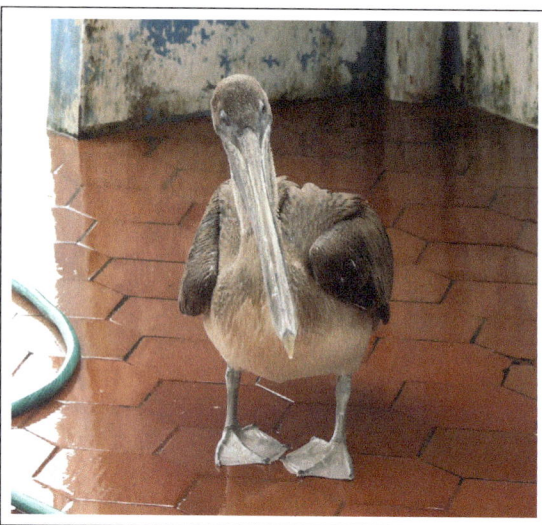

interested in us than in helping the fishermen, while the women tried to buy and sell as the men were looking after their crates of fish, boats and nets.

The fishwives at Santa Cruz Quay, Galápagos were similarly joined by pelicans as well as sea lions, these creatures were

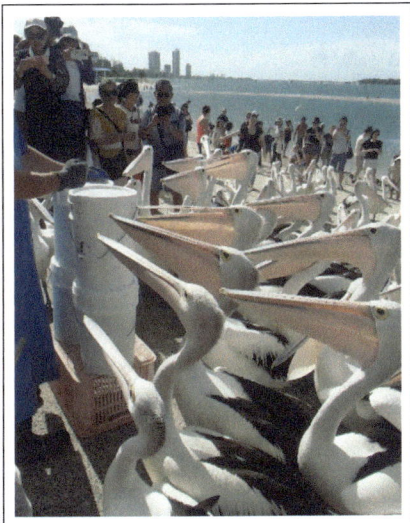

also so professional at their clearing duties!

On a different *scale* altogether, the fish-market shop and restaurant on the beach at Coolangatta, Gold Coast, Australia was a tremendous experience. With so many guts and bones to dispose of, the explanation was right out there on the beach. Every afternoon at 4pm staff came out with an enormous quantity of buckets to throw their contents to the waiting pelicans. These had learned very quickly to come for their daily freebie and lined-up amusingly once they saw the possibility of action. Tourism had caught on too, coachloads of Japanese and Chinese were there pushing to the front with their cameras, umbrellas, hats and gloves ready for action – only to be right in the firing line of the flying 'guts'. Thank goodness not to belong to a pushy nation! The sight of the pelican's

synchronized beaks moving left and right as the fish entrails 'flew' was hilarious: a sight to enjoy.

Most of the African countries I have visited have what are amusingly called the 'Bottoms-up Boutiques', these being clothes sent from the 1st

world and sold, laid out along the roadside and requiring the ladies to bend 90 degrees, or further, to find their requirements. In Darjeeling, I was disturbed that the contents of the giant bales of clothes were generally picked up by the more affluent locals who took them home, improved the goods in the best way they could before putting them back on the market, making a fair living. The poorest never had a look in!

Other markets in Africa, especially South Africa, are particularly fun to visit. Bartering for basketware, bead and wire work or simple carved goods is always such fun – whether you need the items or not! Craft markets come in endless guises too!

One 'craft market' was at a stall way out in the countryside in Namibia where a traditionally dressed Herero woman was selling dolls dressed similarly. They were lovely but my days of collecting foreign dolls were well over – sadly for her. The young lads selling rocks were not our scene either but the pineapples near St Lucia in KwaZulu-Natal were just up our street, a big bowl full for about £1.

When visiting Rwanda to see the gorillas we visited a school whose students were mostly orphans after the terrible genocide. These children had

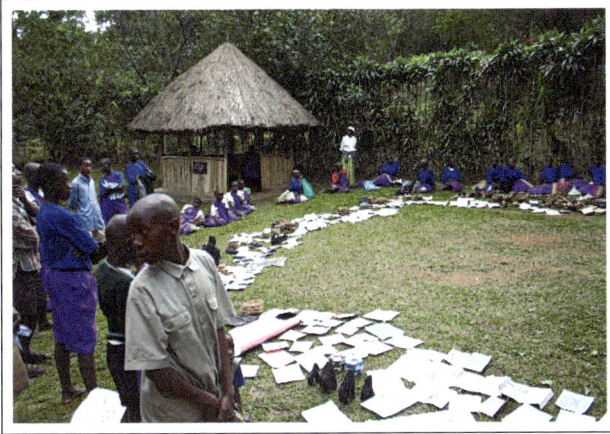

been so busy carving gorillas as well as making drawings of them, all for sale – I treasure my purchases and the memory of those smiling faces as well as their exuberant dancing.

It took a good 30 minutes to bargain through our coach window for an embroidered wall-hanging and a dozen roundels. I wasn't worried whether I purchased them

or not, but I did have a requirement for some prizes so continued for the sheer fun. The haggling continued, my fellow bus passengers were most certainly entertained, and finally the ladies outside came down and down with their pricing to a figure that was both fair and realistic; we were all happy and had had a lot of camaraderie, amusement and photographs along the way!

I sailed the South Pacific on a Chinese cargo ship, which, although it had passengers, was most important by being the Tuamotu Atolls and Marquesas Islands' corner shop. When we stopped to offload and upload, we would go ashore and visit for as long as the work allowed.

Every island had their individual crafts and were very happy to sell. There were atolls specializing in the pearls grown within the splendid waters of these sunken volcanoes. Some islands created amazing wood carvings and decorated oyster shells; others offered their paintings on both homemade paper and parchment (known as 'tapa'). The silk work as well as flower creations were sensational. The market at Hiva Oa, Pacific home to both Paul Gauguin and Jacques Brel was remarkable, both in its simplicity

and variety. On what appeared to be washing lines around the village green, hung enormous painted 'tablecloth' sized sheets: many with Gauguin-styled artwork. There were also garlands, head-dresses, earrings, scarves, necklaces, patchwork and bone and wood carvings laid out on the ground or low tables. We all had a ball!

Way up the River Napo in Ecuador we visited a bush market which was both interesting and most disturbing. There were modern goods for sale such as CDs, radios, shampoo and plastic goods alongside buckets of wriggling mopane worms – our guide showed us how to eat them, but we declined to try! There were various unidentifiable fish

and leaves but sadly bushmeat too. It was quickly made evident that we were not wanted there, so we stayed a very short while. Then, before returning to our dugout, we were horrified to come across a baby howler monkey for sale close to a mound of raw meat. Its mother was obviously a part of the meat for sale. Hard though it is, I always have to remember the difference in cultures and their way of survival but the memory of that visit has remained uneasily in my mind.

Travelling to Otavalo while still in Ecuador, we gave a lift to three girls who were on their way to the famous market. Otavalo has a long history of craft from wool through cotton, silk and wood. This is reputably the best textile area and the base of their economy. There were stalls selling so many handmade clothes, crafts and the famous Panama hats. We

enjoyed wandering around purchasing a few things and feasting our eyes on the beautiful and very happy people.

Interestingly unlike Bolivia the women rarely don a hat, the married ones now wear a cloth around their 'ponytail' having dispensed with the Panama worn in times past.

From the simplicity of the use of an abacus in Zhigazi and Lhasa, Tibet I travelled to Chengdu, Sichuan, China where I wandered through the street

market that had every live creature possible for sale, be it turtle, snake, dog, cat, bird, insect, fish, you name it – it was bound to have been there. Above and beside were songbirds of all kinds in tiny cages, not far from all the spices, herbs, fruits and vegetables. Oh my, that was a revelation as well as a cocktail of aromas! Back then in 1987 I had never seen anything like it.

Most of the streets of Hong Kong at that time were very similar, retail-retail-retail in the gutter, on the path and within the buildings; all the goods were mass produced in the sweatshops above. Advertising placards, electric wires and washing lines, all hung above and alongside the many cages of songbirds.

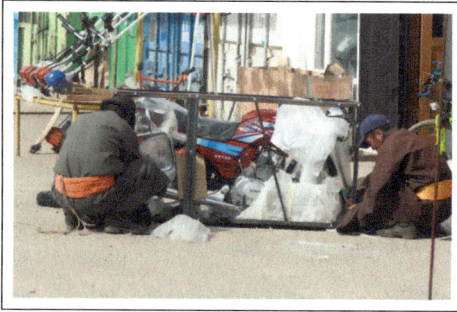

In 2017, far more recently, we had been travelling across the Gobi Desert, the Steppe and finally came into Karakorum town, with its very modern make-do market.

There the whole area covering about two acres was a grid of old containers. They were most efficiently arranged beside each other, with easy access and as always, a multitude of diverse items for sale. Again, the people were charming and welcoming. I watched as two young fellows eagerly took ownership of a brand-new motorbike, and to see them busy working their way through all the packaging was great fun. Amazing what came out of those 'container shops'!

At the stalls beside the Erdene Zuu Monastery I bartered for two pairs of local handmade 'felt' shoes for my great-nieces – aged then one and three. The little shoes turned out to be a resounding success, so warm as they were made of cashmere – later to be handed on!

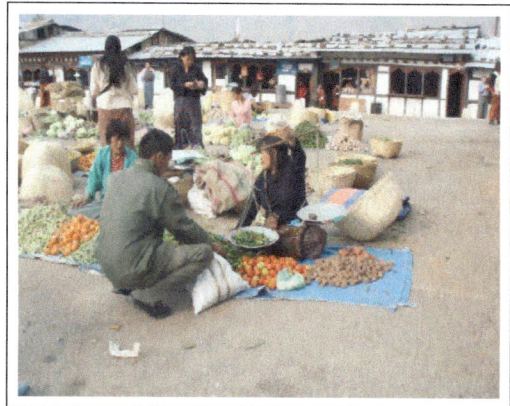

The markets I experienced on my first trip to Bhutan in 1998 were very simply a collection of ladies selling the goods they had produced from their farm, garden patch

or in the home. Everything was so fresh; they were all so welcoming and such fun, and no sign of plastic, nor at that time was there TV, mobile phone or modernity as we know it. Since then, understandably, things have changed.

Often there would be a stall beside a check post as we travelled across that wonderful country. The check was needed usually only to confirm that no wood was aboard; the cutting and removing of the woodland is not allowed, only dead wood may be utilized, and incidentally, every school child is required to plant a tree on the King's birthday. The stalls would have strings of Yak cheese, local fruit, vegetables, or nuts for sale.

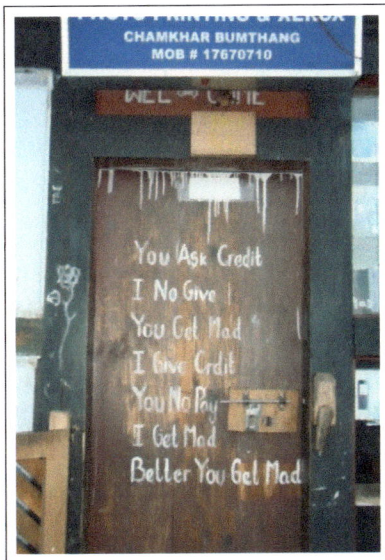

Shop signs are always good for a laugh!

The largest market in Thimpu, the capital, was down beside the river with a few roofed areas but mostly open to the elements. However, by my last visit (2010) a brilliant new covered brick-built market in the centre of town had been constructed and was buzzing with activity – needless to say, with neon lights, plastic mobile phones and yes, television had arrived too!

Able to purchase our needs at the New Zealand farmers' markets was fun, similarly in Lancaster, Pennsylvania where the Amish sell some of their produce in a sophisticated covered market. Both Larkspur, San Francisco and Annapolis, Maryland have been fun to visit also. French street markets are always busy places with all the local cheeses, wines, fruit and vegetables

there for purchasing, along with of course the local crops, be it lavender, sunflowers or basketware from a specialist basket maker. I use a basket daily purchased at such a market made by a Mauritanian living in that area – I love it.

The stall selling Russian dolls and hats was another fun time experienced on a visit to St Petersburg, also a Sámi handicraft market in Northern Norway too. Sadly, none of these were up for the traditional bartering although I tried as usual!

The most incredible fish market I have ever visited was the Tokyo fish market and tuna auction, the 'Tsukiji' auction (May 2010). We learned that only two groups of 70 visitors were allowed through each morning on a first come, first enter basis. We left our hotel at 1am and were easily the first by some 90 minutes. The 'queue' which was just us of course at this stage, was out in the street with no sitting area at all. However, the two of us used the three plus hours to our benefit, taking it in turn to keep our position and to wander around the extremely busy fish and sundry stands. There was every fish and mollusk possible for sale: alive, dead, dried, prepared and packaged for instant serving. Cleanliness was paramount and friendliness enormous. We had to look out for market transport, trolleys, forklift trucks, water hoses, ice: dry and solid, the purchasers, the marketeers, the auctioneers and the surfaces. It was both a revelation and a thrill. The actual tuna auction was an eye opener, the frozen fish were coming in by the trolley load steaming with dry ice and then sent slipping across the floor with great ease. The prospective purchasers were going through the ritual of testing the tail meat for quality: this involved cutting a small amount from the tail, rubbing it through the fingers like putty and then chewing it before spitting it out to rub it again'!

Gradually the queue out in the street was building up and finally the first 70 were ushered into the hall where we were given yellow vests and instructions. Finally we filed into the Great Auction Hall, where the

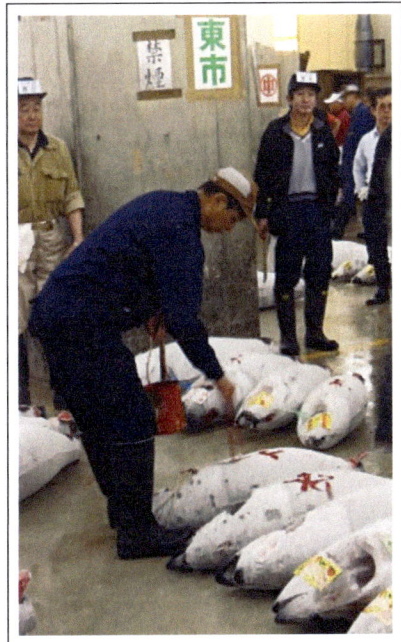

atmosphere was buzzing, and at a prescribed time great hand bells were rung. The auctioneers mounted their orange boxes to start their 'garble'. I had absolutely no idea of the figures, the names or the prices that were uttered but suffice to say that three of them auctioned at the same time, their faces becoming ruddier by the moment. A man stood beside each auctioned fish and immediately painted it with a Japanese Cyrillic message, no doubt the purchaser's identification, and then silence. More activity all around and then once more the bells rang out and the whole process started again. The whole market affair was totally fascinating, an amazing experience even at that early hour – and it was still not 6am when we arrived back in our taxi at the hotel, *fish free*, for breakfast!

One summer back in the early 70s I met my French friend in Nice, where we visited the old town including the street market but my friend said we must visit the market in nearby Ventimiglia, just over the border in Italy. My memory recalls many stalls with endless rails hanging with goods for sale that were mostly made of leather. I was a very happy girl coming home with the latest style of handbag, as well as a brown suede jerkin, again high style of the time! The train journey along the coastline was simply stunning though on a very old train.

Life has moved on, now we appear to have regular car boot sales here as well. Many unwanted goods and clothes are simply moved on; a wonderful form of recycling rather than sending them for landfill. Long may markets continue across the world to save the planet for those trading youngsters.

Chapter 9
Arts and Crafts

There are always surprises when getting under the skin of foreign countries and there is nothing better than to observe the indigenous peoples to see their dress and adornments. Many are specifically traditional to a particular area, sometimes simply a small valley or town. The same observations apply the world over, we only have to think of our own Harris Tweed, Aran knit or Guernsey sweater.

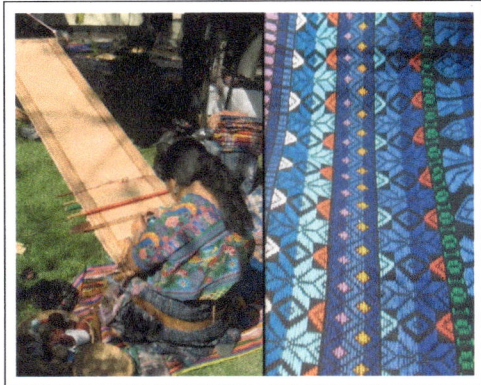

I was so taken by the colourful textiles I found in Guatemala, the cotton thread produced, dyed and then woven on either a backstrap or standing loom, the former used by the Mayan culture – the Spanish arriving with the latter in the 16th century. Much of this cloth is then embroidered in many colours, the design being a very individual style. Each village will specialise in a distinctive colour or pattern resulting in their huipils, a square-shaped blouse and cortes, a panel worn over their skirt, being highly recognizable with techniques and methods passed down through the generations. The Bhutanese too also use the backstrap loom along with their upright one.

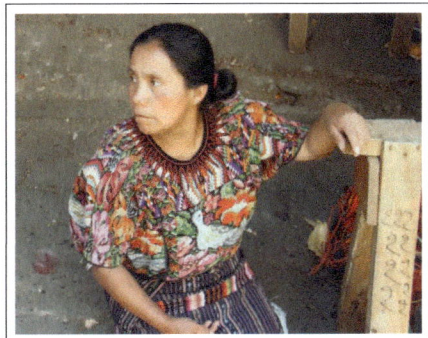

Visiting the Gold Museum in Bogotá, Colombia I was blown away by the intricacy of the gold work created by the pre-Hispanic people of Colombia. These numerous cultures had varying styles but all so intricate and a joy to have them exhibited within such an amazing building. There in Bogotá

I was introduced to Fernando Botero and the museum named after him. We moved from room to room studying his 'fat' paintings and sculptures. At first, I couldn't stop myself laughing at these, as I saw them as cartoon-style artwork. But, after that afternoon and many other occasions seeing his work, I learned to appreciate them enormously. During 2000 Botero had given the nation 123 pieces of his artwork, since when there have been others donated. An amazing collection from their own Colombian artist.

The leatherwork we found at Jericó, in the department of Antioquia, high up in the Colombian hills, was a joy too. As well as saddlery, there were

wonderful belts, bags, sandals and for me a purse in a style I had been looking for over a long period of time, sold to this tourist and used by her ever since!

Pottery is produced in many individual styles, In Zimbabwe a particular group of young ladies and men led by Penelope Vincent, nicknamed Penzo, produce and paint 'one of a kind' highly collectable tableware depicting brightly coloured African wildlife and landscapes. Each piece is individually signed and now sold around the world, as are some

pots, thrown at the side of the road using an old cart wheel in India. In Turkey we could have a go when visiting the tiny village of Avanos, noted for its pottery, ceramics, carpet weaving, tapestry and wine making. Here we were shown intricate designs painstakingly reproduced from the Iznik originals. For once in my life I declined their offer of teaching me, so it wasn't my lump of clay that wobbled and slipped to the side that time!

The crafts I found down in the South Pacific were fabulous, all created from the local produce in methods and styles handed down over the generations. At

the atoll of Fakarava we landed by whale boat, a large flat-bottomed punt-style facility, where we were given gardenias for our hair. Here we could wander at ease along the street of what was the coral rim of a caldera. I had been advised that this atoll was the best place to buy dark pearls, so without haste I headed off to

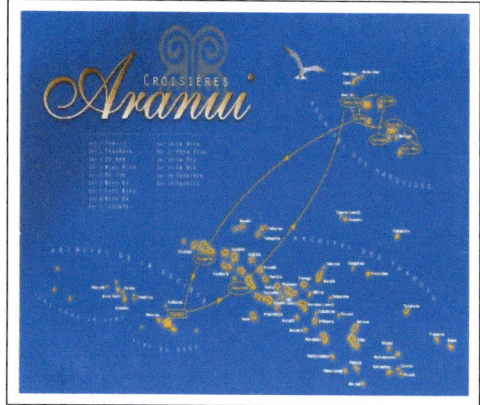

a private house where I found a young girl showing a beautiful display of

her work. Never one to be long about shopping, I was steps ahead of the rest of the passengers! The breeding of pearl oysters in these lagoons produced black marine cultured pearls and are from the black-lip pearl oyster. I watched how intricately a mother of

pearl bead was inserted into the animal together with a piece of tissue (mantle)

taken from another pearl. Instinctively the oyster deposits mother of pearl on the surface of the bead, taking about three years before being ready for harvesting. For larger pearls the process is repeated possibly twice more but generally that is then the

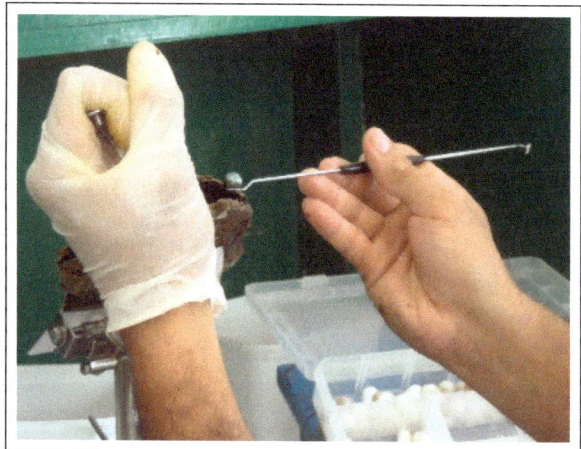

maximum size. Numerous families in this archipelago practice this activity bringing an enormous help to their economy.

Given time on that atoll to study the amazing carvings that these people had created in their church, I began very quickly to learn how talented the people of these South Sea Islands were. The carvings within the Notre Dame Cathedral on Nuku Hiva were staggeringly good. The statues, pulpit and baptismal font were all hewn from local teanu wood; the Stations of the Cross were carved from a single trunk of temanu. Here I found that the Marquesan way of life was woven into the scenes. One station showed the Mount of Olives covered in breadfruit trees, while another showed Christ bothered by a drunkard brandishing a bottle!

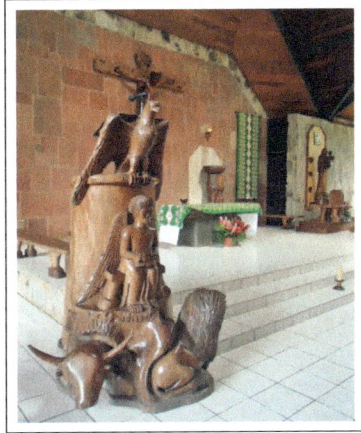

On Hiva Oa there were incredibly intricate necklaces made of oyster shells and carvings too. The painted silk work, embroidery, garlands, earrings, pareos (a wraparound skirt), basket work, bone and wood carvings we found were all top quality.

On Omoa we were welcomed as usual with flowers for our hair before sitting beneath some magnificent trees

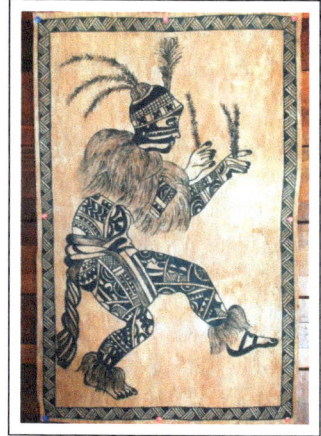

to learn the process of making tapa or bark cloth. Tiaiho, a charming girl, demonstrated her art and explained the use of the different trees. The bark cloth she made was from the inner bark of ute (paper mulberry), aoa (banyan) and mei (breadfruit). Each yields a different colour and texture of tapa, ranging from the finely textured white tapa of ute to the rough, chocolate coloured cloth of banyan. I had to concentrate hard because the heat was high and the rain heavy and we were on a steep learning curve. Using mei, she first stripped the inner bark of a small branch, then placing it on a flat stone to pound with a tapa beater made of hard wood, often toa, she softened the fibres. The bark was folded and beaten flat again, this repeated many times in order to meld the bark fibres together. Finally the flat sheet of tapa was cleaned and dried. A wash of starch is sometimes applied to stiffen and glaze the bark cloth. Only then is a design applied, using a brush dipped in writing ink. The results of their work were magnificent.

Mme Simiona of Omoa also demonstrated the art of making an umukei, a fresh, scented hair piece or corsage made of plants, flowers and spices, worn by the ladies of the islands.

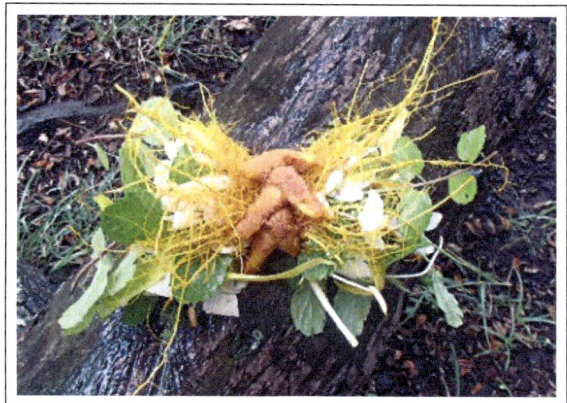

The diversity of craft island to island was similar to the differences found from district to district in Madagascar. One valley people on that amazing Indian Ocean Island may be offering their wood carvings, the next basket ware, another stonework or even nearby within another district, precious stones. One can't help their personal economy all the time, so my standard donation of tennis balls had to suffice frequently!

I was enchanted by the hardy people of the Nikolskoye Village of Bering Island, right at the end of the Commander Island chain, in the Kamchatka District of far east Russia. This subarctic treeless island is desolate in the extreme, covered in a grassy steppe with a coastline that alternates between cliffs with waterfalls and sandy beaches. Its inhabitants were mostly rookeries of seals, other sea mammals and often over a million birds.

With a population of about 800, many Nikolskoyers were employed in the fishing industry, the others either hunting or sadly unemployed. They are divided roughly evenly between Russians and Aluets, and mixing between the two is common. Despite living in an environment that is extremely rich in wildlife, the inhabitants of the island are very restricted in the use of these resources since almost the entire island is a nature reserve. We were most warmly met by the locals and soon learned that we were the first tourists to visit in three years which was no doubt why they were so keen to allow us to

wander at ease amongst their old wooden houses, small gardens with rickety fences, run-down sheds and by all the rusty metal that lay about. There were the inevitable two-storey concrete blocks, underlining the old regime. We could walk along the sea front, which was not as we know it, just a dusty track on which a couple of battered vehicles came by during our visit to find a wonderful statue of Bering, another of a maiden made from metal and a superb one crafted out of driftwood.

More of the locals came out to join us as we proceeded towards their museum and finally into their school hall where both the students and the

villagers, including the elders, gave us a wonderful song and dance concert. Afterwards they offered us some of their craft, mainly quite simple knitting, sewing and painting but I was thrilled to find a tiny basket with lid, just four inches long and made of very fine grass. I treasure that purchase for its fine work in such a tough environment.

We enjoyed calm seas as we sailed into Cumberland Sound to visit the tiny hamlet of Pangnirtung on the south shore of Baffin Island with a population of about 1,500. The name translated from the Inuit word means 'place of the bull caribou'. Here we found the most delightful people, again so happy to have visitors and willing to welcome us into their church, shop and around the few streets. We were warmly greeted by two ladies into their turf house, made of heather and mud. With an interpreter we were invited to sit with the ladies who showed us their sewing and craft tools as well as giving us a wonderful insight into living in such a home. The walls were lined with pages from mail order catalogues, the windows now plastic replaced the traditional gut. Ptarmigan wings are used for sweeping and bleached bones used as toys. Beds used to be made of heather with caribou skins but now they have foam, quilts and even a gas heater. The toilet was elsewhere although with the more modern wooden houses I did notice that they had integral heating

and water including their WC. Most were built high off the ground to accommodate the high volume of winter snow.

The village had a craft shop and gallery as the number of artists within the village is large. Their talent is so good that they have a guild

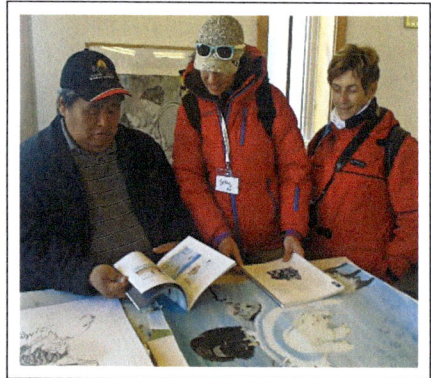

that produces exceptional quality woven tapestries, lithographs, soapstone work, carvings, paintings and rugs. Here I was able to purchase a wedding present from Andrew Qappik, one of their most renowned artists. He was very happy to both sell and talk about his work!

Again, these wonderful people had invited us to their community hall to enjoy some of their singing including the amazing throat singing and dancing,

they insisted that we joined in, which was lovely. Some of the dances were similar to a Scottish reel (strip the willow etc.), brought across the Atlantic by early sailors I expect. They also invited us to enjoy the beluga soup and arctic char soup, both more of a casserole than soup and each served with a small scone – a most delicious offering.

Not quite so remote was the Tlingit village of Kake, between Juneau and Wrangell on the west side of Kupreanof Island. Here one of the Kake elders took us to see the 132ft totem pole, Alaska's largest totem carved from a single tree. I was able to visit the local carver who was making his own totem, he also showed us some of his previous work including bowls, hats and oars.

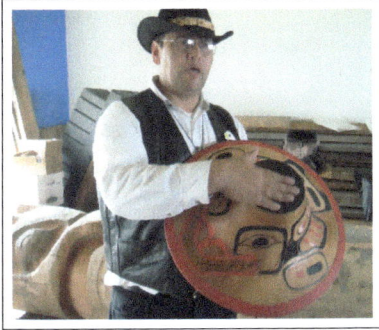

Sur is the boat-building base in Oman. When I visited in 2006 many of the old boats in the harbour were sadly simply wrecks, but I did have a chance to go to a boat-building yard and have a walk amongst the dhows being built. The boatbuilders were very happy to show me what they were doing; most talented men using very little modern machinery.

Balsa wood was carved into local fauna shapes when I visited the Napo Wildlife Reserve on the great Napo River, Ecuador. Here I was enchanted by a young soul of the Huaorani tribe carving away beside the river. I bought a Tamarin monkey and a bird painted delightfully, happily very light for easy transportation, and I have treasured his work ever since.

The Saturday craft market in Durban is fun, we sallied forth one morning to see the extensive beadwork created by the Zulus, their sewn crafts, and some questionable painting!

There were also baskets, wood carvings and many trinkets. Latterly, the children have started working incorporating plastic, recycling bottles and other commodities into their artwork, which is then put for sale, as a double-pronged form of education.

Using a commodity that is in no short supply at the elephant orphanage at Pinnawala Village beside the Oya River in Sri Lanka where we found ourselves outside the 'Elephant Poo Factory'. We couldn't refuse the chance to call in to see how we could assist their economy, money to finance the cost of caring for these young, injured and sometimes blind animals. They were making

paper from the dung and turning it into pads, cards, mobiles and much more.

In Bhutan it is the daphne bush that is used to make paper for similar use as well as carrier bags and wrapping paper. Local flowers are often placed on the

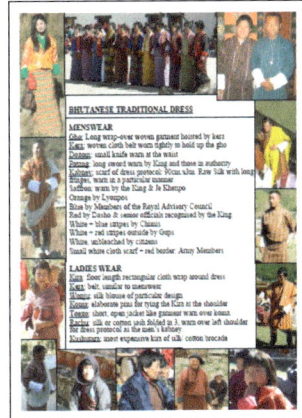

'mash' before drying, offering glorious designs of excellent quality. This is just one of the crafts in Bhutan, their yathra weaving, the silk making, dying and weaving were all exceptional, as was the general weaving of all the cloth used in making the national dress for both women, the kira and for the men, the gho. Basketware, wood carving and artwork are tremendous. Traditionally none of their work is ever signed. As archery is the national sport, bamboo bows are made, along with arrows or reeds, and are fletched with feather vanes. Quivers are made of wood with an animal hide covering and a woven strap. Their talents in the lower-lying lands extended to bamboo work, used for fencing, housing, farming and household baskets as well as even hats.

Ceramics and more particularly tiles seem synonymous with Spain. I was delighted to see the craft at such a high standard at Triana, over the Eiffel Bridge from central Seville. There were two kilns firing as well as many shops selling pottery, ceramics and mosaics of varying size. Many of the markets,

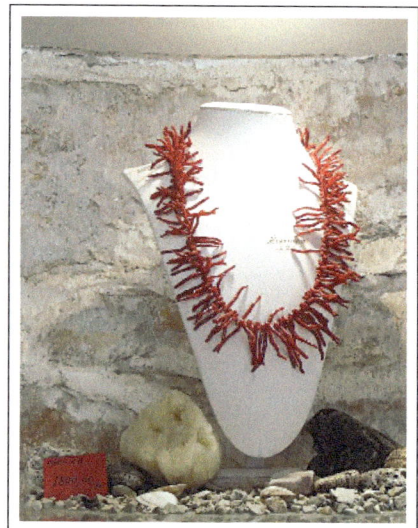

halls and even the stations had walls covered with pictures depicting history, traditions and rural life. In churches too, like the Moorish Revival Chapel of El Carmen's dome, the mosaics continued, showing Carmen's coat of arms. At Pinhão, even the station had amazing tiles depicting the area.

When visiting the island of Zlarin off the Croatian coast I was thrilled to meet Mala, the last gentleman still working with the famed coral of that area. Sadly he finds that no one wants to train to continue this tradition using the fabulous coral only found in their local waters. Losing these crafts is such a sadness, they are all so individual and certainly not something that one can learn from a book. This loss and that of so many crafts across the world, many in our own Country, has to be helped and reversed.

Chapter 10

Restaurants

Whether a café, restaurant or dining room, travelling certainly offers a tremendous opportunity to sample the specialities of a particular country. When not self-catering I always love to try these and have enjoyed many, though some of course have turned out to be questionable and others – well, shall we say challenging!

When meeting friends in Montevideo we were taken to a restaurant called 'Los Tahlatis' meaning 'little boards' as traditionally food was always served on scrubbed wooden boards. Starters were of offal and sausage followed by steak or lamb of which Uruguay has plenty. This was a great start to our five-week South American adventure back in 1980.

Once in Buenos Aires we were invited to dine with two Russian lawyers who took us to a beautiful restaurant where all the meat was cooked outside on the restaurant frontage on BBQ stakes over a charcoal open fire. Here we were introduced to Civite (kid goat) which was extremely tender and then Asado (beef), good but less tender.

As we began our bus trip across Argentina towards Bolivia and onwards to Peru our eating places became more basic and far more amusing if not challenging!

Many times, we chose to self-cater by simply purchasing avocados and oranges as they had good thick skins, dulce de leche, cheese and even a tin of peaches! But often our choice was the only café in a one-horse town!

In Tucumán we were invited to a 'Pena', a local folklore centre where we enjoyed a meal of tamales (meat and cereal in leaves), a steak and salad followed by a rather nasty cheese pancake with treacle! Happily, the traditional music along with the unmistakable singing voices of the Latin Americans was fabulous.

At La Quiaca we stayed at a hotel that was more comfortable than expected but we did have to go out to a restaurant to eat. As the group of us sat at long trestle tables we were amused to find that one popular dish was subjected to a price rise by a considerable number of pesos: the restaurateur, right in front of our very eyes, was not shy to take down the menu display board and put up the higher price! Understandable as they did have a 98% inflation rate at that time!

Across Bolivia the Indians bake in mud ovens called Pelazos right outside their houses. At one point we stopped for a couple of ladies to come aboard our bus to sell their pelazo-baked sponge cakes made from local flour, butter and eggs; they were 10 pesos for three, we bought three and found them very good indeed.

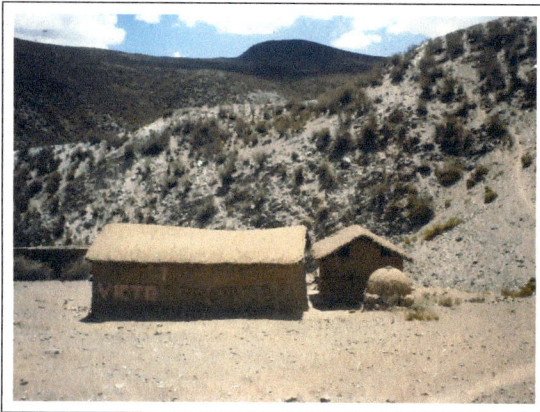

At one small overnight town a group of us decided that we fancied a pizza. The restaurant had tables outside which on a very hot evening suited us well. We sat chattering and watching the world go by while eating our slices of goodness, initially not realising that the neon striplights above were drawing every moth and insect in the district which, once they hit the light, fell below right onto our supper. Never to be forgotten and much laughed about since; it really wasn't mixed herbs sprinkled over as we thought.

Travelling in Chile we found ourselves further north in the Atacama, happily wandering into the village for dinner where we found a local restaurant that looked just fine. It was the first time in my life that I have been totally unable to communicate with the staff or understand anything written on the menu. Finally, I went with the waitress to the kitchen fridge and pointed at what I would like cooked; there wasn't much of a choice so chicken local style had to suffice! We later learned the owners and staff at this particular establishment spoke an individual dialect – they had certainly given us some fun!

Also in the Atacama, we visited the geysers and were able to cook the eggs and heat the milk for our breakfast in the ground – that most certainly was a first!

Way back in the mid '60s I was invited to a fabulous ball in central Paris, after which we went on to the Flower Market whose cafés were famed for their 'soupe à l'oignon' served with thick cheese on the top and croutons. Along with the marketeers and florists we all enjoyed the fun with several of us finishing up dancing on the tables. All good fun at 6am in evening dresses!

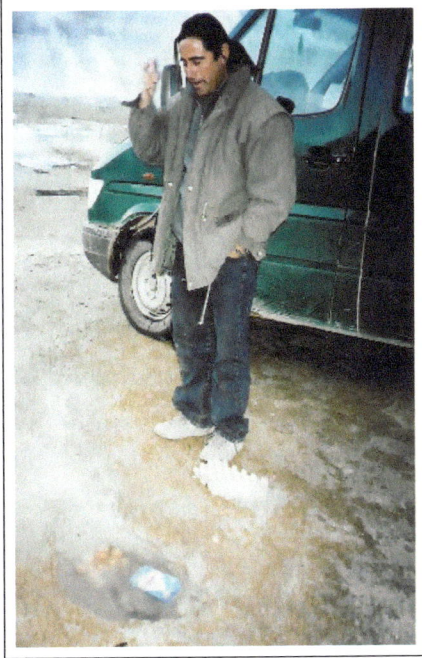

More dancing came as a surprise when we visited the amazing Andres Carne de Res restaurant in Chia, Colombia. We had driven out of Bogotá to visit friends and having had a tour of their glorious house and gardens we trundled down the hill to the village where we were booked into a unique restaurant. Oh my, if I am termed a hoarder, I am in the kindergarten class compared with the owner of this eating house. The staff wore calf-leather aprons with their names on the back. Bric-a-brac lay simply everywhere. Rustic chairs, tables, plates and mugs decorated the

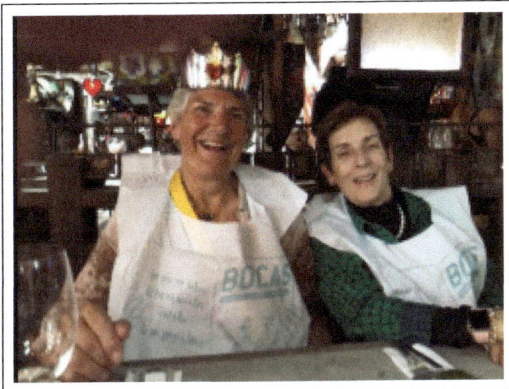

room; the wine came from pottery carafes within a painted bucket with ice and herbs or flowers; starters of black pudding, tripe and chorizo were served on a board, followed by steak and salad, followed by a pudding that appeared to be a very thick junket served with a thick caramel – naughty but scrummy! Only then did the staff come out amongst the tables dancing and playing local instruments. Anyone who had come a distance or had a special occasion was given a crown and sash to wear, and oh yes, they found me!

When sailing on the *Aranui 3* amongst the Marquesas Islands we landed at Ua Huka to deliver their orders and collect their copra etc., before sailing onto Vaipae'e and then to Hane. At Hane we were taken to Fourneir's Restaurant for lunch. This was on the edge of a glorious, wooded area alive with fabulous birds including ultramarine lorikeets and Iphis monarchs. Madame Celine Fournier's speciality is Marquesan goat served barbecued or curried in coconut milk. We enjoyed both along with salads and other vegetables. Another delicacy of the area is langouste, the spiny rock lobster (*panulirus penicillatus*) that live in the many underwater caves surrounding the island.

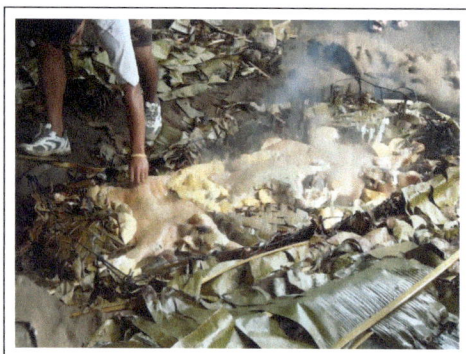

Sadly, I didn't see any at our table!

On the island of Nuku Hiva, we arrived at Chez Yvonne's to enjoy the house speciality which is pork cooked in a native earth oven 'umu'. A wood fire heats volcanic rocks for several hours; the pig and red bananas are wrapped in 'ti' leaves, placed on the red-hot rocks, covered in more banana leaves, burlap sacks and soil. After cooking the contents are carefully removed from the bed in the coals, cut up and served with coconut milk. This was a variation to the 'pigs in blanket' we know so well! We were also given local goat that

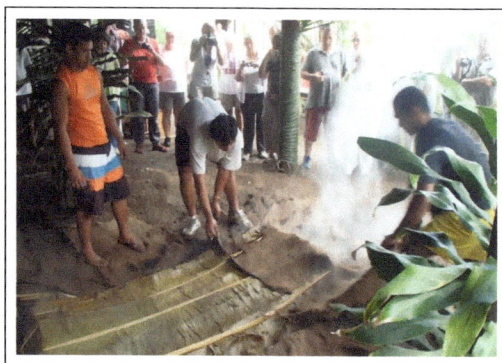

had been cooked above soil; most of us preferred this – with all the beer, merriment and sunshine we were very happy adventurers.

Needless to say, in Southern Africa game is often on the menu and beautifully served. I took a chance when visiting the crocodile farm in St Lucia, KwaZulu-Natal and chose one of the 'inhabitants' for dinner! Apparently, they only use the tail, which was very good, a little like pork but surprisingly quite salty.

When we stayed on the estancia called Zuletta in Ecuador we were offered their speciality, and as in Bolivia it is guinea pig. I had not eaten it the first time it was offered so this time it was a definite yes! When the creature arrived roasted and carved it tasted rather like roast rabbit but with a slight pork flavour. Our experiences up at this glorious house and estate were fabulous;

here we were able to ride up into the mountains to look for spectacled bears (failed!) but we did see many condors which was a true delight.

The famous South African potjoi is always a must, we have enjoyed so many recipes cooking in what looks like a 'witches cauldron' over the hot ashes of an outdoor fire. While staying up in the Drakensberg Mountains we were able to leave it cooking away while going off on a good hike, to return to enjoy immediately after the gin and tonics had been poured out!

In Norway when travelling with the Sámi, reindeer was always on the menu in one form or another. I love it and am happy whichever way they choose to cook it. Eating traditionally in the lavu

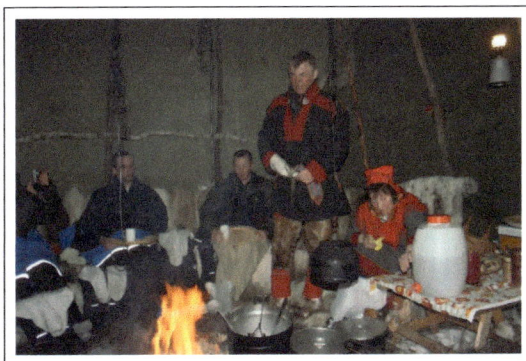

was such fun seated on reindeer skins! Their salmon too, so fresh and flavoursome. We were served it straight from the stake cooked beside the open fire 'lavu-style'!

Coming to restaurants nearer home, a visit to London as a teenager would often include Lyons Corner House at Charing Cross. Later a visit nearly always included Manzi's, the famous fish restaurant; but more recently I was invited to dine at the Ritz during Queen Elizabeth II's Diamond Jubilee celebrations. On the night of the jubilee, we were invited

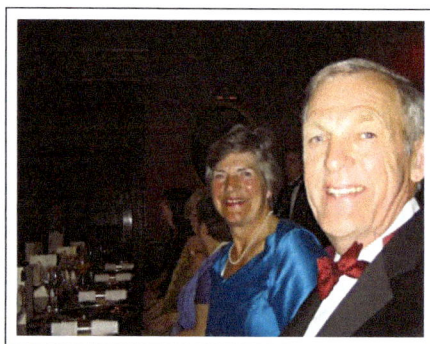

to drinks in the Queen Elizabeth Room before entering the newly decorated William Kent dining room for a spectacular celebratory dinner. Twenty-two of us enjoyed the most wonderful menu, along with accompanying wines and camaraderie in this stunning room. Equally the Ritz Casino restaurant is very special indeed.

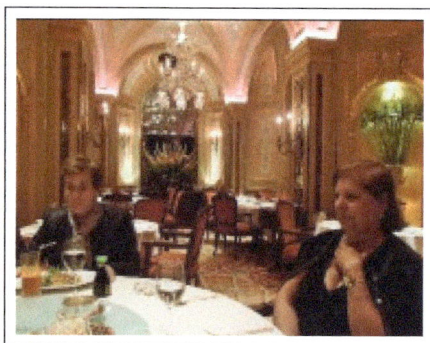

In July 1989 I was invited to the Bicentennial celebrations in Paris and to the Garden Party at Le Palais de l'Élysée by Mme Delachenal, sister of the then President Mitterrand. The weather was wonderful as were the surroundings and hospitality.

Much later, I was again invited when Madame received the Légion d'honneur, a feast to remember and enjoy with all her family and friends.

Another unexpected invitation was to the dinner after enjoying the Passing Out Parade at the NDA, Puna, India. It was all a spectacle with so many traditions and celebrations. Yes, medals were worn!

We were also invited to the commandant's office, an honour indeed.

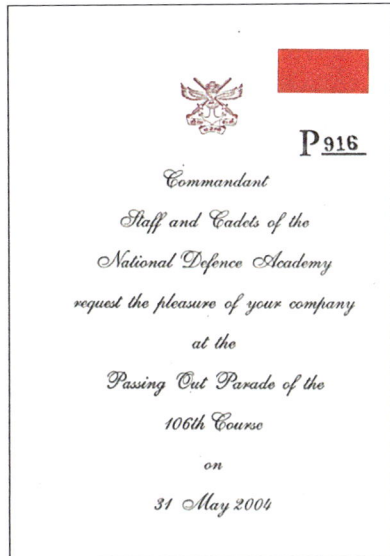

P 916

Commandant
Staff and Cadets of the
National Defence Academy
request the pleasure of your company
at the
Passing Out Parade of the
106th Course
on
31 May 2004

Being welcomed into homes, whether bomas, Rondavals lavu's, yurts, tents, houses or shacks has always been a delight to me – just as I love going into cellars, attics and towers of big houses!

Away from luxury and high-living, but every bit as welcoming, we were entertained at breakfast by a bushman's family in the Kalahari Desert, taken into a Maasai boma in Kenya, and to several traditional houses in Ethiopia, which are amazing. Dinner eaten in Sámi's lavu as well as a Mongolian's

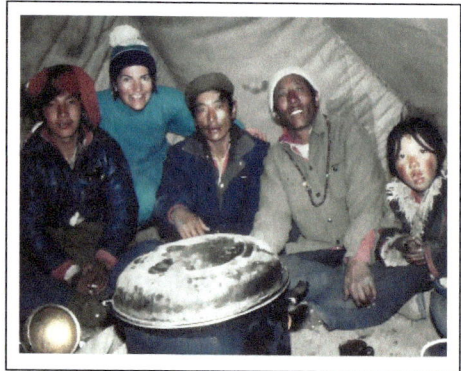

yurt and a form of tea with yak's milk drunk in a Tibetan's tent were equally agreeable.

In Darjeeling our guide was Jamling Tenzing Norgay, son of Sherpa Tensing, who was so excited when we accepted the invitation to go to his house for tea to meet his wife, child and extended family. This was the home of Sherpa Tensing who was the first to climb Everest along with Edmund Hillary. I remember well the stunning view of the mountains from their front room.

Further east at the Imperial Hotel, Tokyo, my travel companion and I were invited to a traditional Tea Ceremony by our Japanese friend. She had brought her friend whose family owned one of the last wholesale kimono businesses called 'Bakurocha' along with the kimonos they were going to dress us in. What fun it was to learn about all the various components of this very special outfit. Once completed and after much laughter I teetered in my Zori sandals & Tabi socks to the lobby for a photograph. From there we 'teetered' on to the Tea House where we were introduced to our Mistress of

Ceremonies at the Ceremonial Hall, walking on the stepping stones through the combed gravel out into the tiny, neat Japanese garden before entering the Tea Room itself. This was a beautiful 'box' shaped room made of bamboo, raised up 20 inches with a small door space where I had to double myself up to enter. The reason for this tradition was apparently to stop the Samurai from entering with their swords. Sitting back on our heels (not easy for MEW) the ceremony proceeded with great tradition and friendliness, the tea being given so much attention and respect. The experience was mind blowing, we enjoyed every cup of tea, titbit and moment. Our Mistress of Ceremonies afterwards told us that in 40 years of overseeing these occasions we were the first 'tourists' to arrive in traditional dress – it made her day and ours.

I could go on for pages about my eating experiences, but before ending this chapter I must include the memories of finding a scorpion beautifully cooked within my roll when dining at the Hilton in Cairo back in 1966. Then there are the joys of dining on game in Africa – kudu, ostrich, eland and boerewors – or the 'restaurant' in Ethiopia where we could order anything at all as long as it was egg.

One simply has to smile and nod appreciatively! How well I remember the steaks in Ireland, and the rabbit casserole in Isola, France and being raised from my bunk during a very rocky sea-passage across the Drakes Passage to enjoy the last reindeer from South Georgia. That was the last of the herd that had been introduced by the whalers, which, along with the rats, had finally been culled and exterminated to allow the endemics to thrive again. But for that the South Georgian Pintail and the South Georgian Pipit might not still be seen. Thankfully their numbers are finally increasing.

Some good news at last.

Chapter 11
Hotels

Hotels come in as many shapes and sizes as do the clients that use them. In a perfect world the requirements should suit both sides which is a major challenge for both traveller and provider. To have a sense of humour and flexibility in one's attitude is often a bonus!

Much humour was required at the Tibetan Zhangmu Hotel above the Happy Bridge on the Nepal/Tibet border, and there were many jokes over the requirement to remove our shoes because of the carpets – they were dire! '1-watt bulbs', no running water, cold and as I learned the following morning when daylight arrived, I most certainly hadn't been the first in the bed. But that was back in 1987 and we all survived. Our hotel in Sikkim was the coldest ever, even colder than the most wonderful Ice Hotel near Kirkenes, Norway that four of us stayed in prior to our reindeer migration trip. Arriving in the evening the 'hotel' was floodlit, and as we wandered into the foyer we found an absolute wonderland which included the reception, the bar with seats, sofa and then even a wedding chapel all made of ice. From this area hung two antler chandeliers in the corridors lighting our way to the bedrooms, each with a curtained archway rather than a door. The 'facilities' both toilet and shower room, restaurant and stores were at least 150 yards away across the snow but all extremely cosy and well appointed.

After dinner, having had instructions on how to use our top-tog sleeping bags and the use of the reindeer mats I was off to my ice bed, though even before I reached my 'room' I was on my bottom; but this igloo bedroom was a new experience.

The bed was normal, but the floor, walls and bedhead, base and sides were all made of 'snice' a mixture of snow and ice. The snice is sprayed over a large balloon for up to two days during mid-December to produce each room, with a circular gap in the top of the roof to allow both light and air. This was perfect and allowed me to see that the sun was coming up when nature required me at 4.30am to wander out to the 'facilities', once having extricated my way out of the bag and with warm clothes retrieved from its depths, I stepped onto the reindeer skin mat to don my snow boots. The early April dawn was indeed a magnificent sight with a pillar of red backlighting the frost on the silver birch forest. There had been a two-inch fall of snow overnight, the hoar frost and the glistening of the whole area was more than enough to take one's breath away: awesome. With a cup of tea, it was back to my igloo for a few more hours! The others all quietly enjoyed their own peace in this world at -4°C. I returned 14 months later to visit Kora, the hotelier at the then melted Ice Hotel and Lars Peter our great skidoo-leader of the migration who by then was much into diving for king crabs. Out we went with him to catch our dinner, the greatest fun and glory be, those crabs are vast!

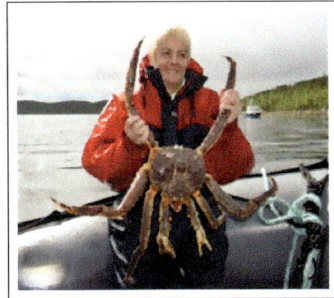

Crossing South America with Pennworld (now Explore) in 1980 was a challenge hotel wise. We always had to try to arrive in good time as although booked in, the hoteliers would often sell the rooms to the first to show up. A nightmare for our guide, but amazingly a bed of a kind was found every night. These hotels varied from basic to quite good, but we were not expecting the Ritz so were generally very happy guests. Right at the end of this five-week trip my travelling companion and I booked into a hotel quite near Miami Airport for three nights to rest up before flying home. This was the first time I was given a card to enter the room, but sadly the following morning, when returning after breakfast, we found that it wouldn't let us in. At reception we were told we hadn't paid for any further use which of course we had. From then on one had to remember not to leave it in the room or (if there are two of you) to request a further card. We have now become so accustomed to the use of cards for lights too, but problems still occur as I experienced in Sri

Lanka when arriving at the Cinnamon Gateway Hotel beside the Negombo Lagoon outside Colombo. Everything was lovely and highly suitable but for our booking being under my name. W is always among the last to receive the key which is therefore generally the furthest from the reception. We walked, walked and walked some more to our room only to find the card key didn't work. After a long flight that is the last thing one wants but yes, it happens, and one must just smile and kick on. More recently at an overnight stay in Windhoek, after breakfast I stayed to fill up our water bottles while my friend returned to the room. Oh dear, I had forgotten that a card was required for the lift too, result: grounded!

Walk and walk again we did at the most gargantuan hotel I have ever stayed at. This was the Mockba 'Russian-style' hotel in St Petersburg. The dining room was similar to an army mess and the hike to the rooms according to my roommate was equal to a par four with an added bank of lifts to wait patiently at! We soon learned not to forget anything before going out on our daytrips because time would most certainly not allow a return to the room!

During the early 90s a friend and I visited Venice at the beginning of January, a cold place indeed at that time of the year with all the water and mist. Our old palace converted to hotel was fun except for the size of our room – minuscule – and even more so, the size of the bathroom which I believe must have been the 'hat cupboard'. How we laughed at our situation, we were able to 'sit upon', with hands in the basin and feet in the shower, so small was our en-suite! On that same trip I had stayed at a hotel in Oberlech where I was given a single room that was also tiny, where the heat was horrendously high with no controls and no window either. They had no other room to offer me – that was an awful week for one who generally sleeps with the window wide open. Again, the most ridiculous 'hole' I was initially given was in Ooty, India. There are many pitfalls to single rooms – this room was at the back of the hotel right beside the kitchen bins, again with no window. Back I went to the guide who offered me his room, which was masses better than mine – but still I complained, explaining the amount of money I had paid for a single room, I discovered it was more than he earned in a month. The result was that I was given the Maharaja's room at the hotel in Bangalore complete with a lad sitting outside my door to fetch anything I required. That suite was so large I felt I should put my dressing gown on to walk from the four-poster bed to the bathroom, but it also had a large balcony on which I held a drinks party (BYOB) for my fellow travellers on our last evening – well I did have the staff! Heyho.

Another nightmare is arriving at the hotel's reception after a very long journey to find that they have lost your booking and there is no room available. This happened to a friend and I on a business trip to Toronto. At first, they told us we must find somewhere else, but after a while they relented as it was very late and somehow found us a most sub-standard room for the rest of the night. The following day we were given the accommodation that had been booked for us – I remember well the great heated cabinet that arrived each morning with our room-service breakfast complete with 'full English' and fresh warm blueberry muffins, yummy.

However, arriving at the very end of the Transpantaneira, Porto Jofre, Brazil we finally boarded our tiny boats to go to our accommodation, which was supposed to be a brand new 'camp-style hotel'. It was only then that we and our guide learned that there was absolutely no camp and were delivered instead to a houseboat half an hour up the river. The owner, Charles, had let us down badly, our leader Santiago, far more so. We stayed that one night on this dire floating dump before a satisfactory hotel was provided, be it far

away from where we should have been. We pulled together and gave Charles a darn good dressing down which he truly deserved, and thankfully this certainly didn't stop anyone of us from thoroughly enjoying our trip.

Arriving in the dark at our hotel in Ulaanbaatar, Mongolia, again after an exceedingly long pair of flights, we found the hotel's front door locked.

Our driver sent me around the side to the staff entrance – this I felt was most questionable, 'Was it a brothel'? came to mind, the rest of our group said that if I failed to return within 10 minutes they would come after me, but happily I discovered someone who was expecting us. We received an eleventh floor, basically furnished, rectangular concrete unit with glass on two full sides, thick blanket-style curtains and exhibition-standard carpeting, all in matching grey but it was thankfully equipped with a comfortable utility bed and pillow.

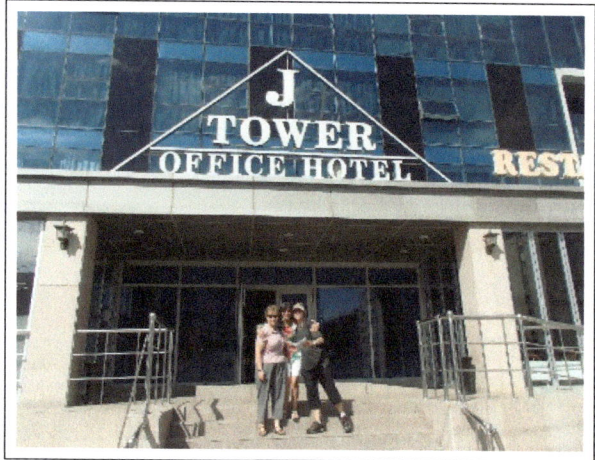

The overnight accommodation in Oslo was minimalist, extremely comfortable and spotlessly clean, the breakfast the following morning being a typical Scandinavian buffet of fine good hotel fare which suited us well. An overnight stay in Ottawa too was most comfortable, though we were most amused by the completely do-it-yourself breakfast, the egg chef being the only member of staff on duty. Signs instructed us to collect every single item from the various fridges, shelves and cupboards, enjoy it and then put all the packaging in the recycle, or unwanted food into the waste bin, and then the washing up on the trolley. After that the rest of the day was our own!

124

Luxury awaited us at our most convenient hotel, Sutton Place Hotel in Vancouver. I was happy to crash out in our extremely comfortable room after yet another long journey. My roommate was still firing on all cylinders so popped out for dinner while I was out for the count in a trice but even with earplugs, I was awakened at 2am by a spasmodic bell in the corridor and so, after a while, I checked, finding a couple of sleepyheads doing the same. Seemingly there was the sound of pouring water in the lift shaft, the lift had stopped working and no one was answering the phone, so we all went back to bed! Now it was my time to fire on all cylinders and at 6am I was ready for a swim. With my roommate still dead to the world I crept out only to find the lift still out of operation and on returning to the room the electronic key failed to allow me back in. No choice but to walk the 16 flights down to the reception and then up two more to the pool. To top it all I didn't realise that the same key would open the ladies changing rooms. All the facilities were fabulous and having enjoyed each

one I went straight to breakfast expecting my roommate to be there. No sign of her and even after numerous calls I failed to contact her. She had chosen a different dining room and had also been locked out of our room. She had heard the phone ringing but of course was in the corridor. Once again, we were both required to climb the 16 flights back up, return to the reception for a new key and climb those steps again. Returning that afternoon, with relief, we were able to use the staff lift, but the following morning when leaving the hotel, we had to bring our luggage (yes) down all those stairs. Even so with all that we had the most wonderful time in Vancouver, such an interesting city and the hotel staff, with their continuing nightmare, were kindness itself.

In March 2007 we had reached Gangtey, Bhutan. We visited the village before driving further up the valley to the chalet-style guest house situated on the hillside overlooking the marshes where the black-neck cranes stay over the winter months. The guest house owner had just completed the build and was keen to improve anything to make his visitors both more comfortable as well as suitable for the birdwatchers and general tourists alike. Bless him, he explained that being illiterate and untravelled he felt at a disadvantage and requested that we give him any advice possible. The en-suite rooms were comfortable, even if the bed was somewhat hard for me, the homemade wooden doors and fittings creaked but with earplugs they were well silenced! The local potatoes we were given at dinner were simply the best, so much so we requested them for breakfast too. I wished the gentleman well. When the flora and fauna of that area is so exciting, the lack of a plug or bright light is immaterial. Bhutan, and especially this district, is a true Shangri La.

To stay at the colonial Windamere Hotel on Observatory Hill, Darjeeling, the original Heritage House of the Himalayas, is experience enough if only to call in for tea. Built in 1841 and later frequented by the British tea planters it still presented a perfect afternoon tea, which we were thrilled to enjoy. We received cucumber sandwiches, cake, tea made with tea leaves and served by a waitress wearing a lacy apron, all while enjoying the sound of the resident pianist. Our room had an open fire, lit and cared for by the staff, old-fashioned beds, a great experience to enjoy. As we were leaving the staff were busy preparing for the stars and film crew to arrive, including the great Peter Ustinov. Darn it, we were there just a day too soon!

Another historic hotel is the Victoria Falls Hotel in Zimbabwe. Built by the British back in 1904, it was originally conceived as accommodation for workers on the Cape-to-Cairo railway. The position near to the falls themselves gives a perfect view of the rising spray. Cecil Rhodes insisted that the first bridge over the mighty Zambezi should be built in a place that the spray would fall on the passing trains, which is why the site is so near to the 'Boiling Pot'. The present décor of the hotel

is still very colonial with great armchairs, sofas and standard lamps; large paintings and photographs of famous visitors including the visit of our Royal Family in 1947. Some new wings have been added and most recently the outdoor breakfast area and the pool. Our room was small, quaint

with four-poster single beds, mosquito nets, chintz curtains and an air-conditioning system that was very noisily trying to do better! The staff were excellent, helping us enjoy our one night stay enormously.

Another old hotel Jude and I stayed at was the Monastery Hotel of St Francis de Santiago, Santiago de Compostela which was a converted monastery right next to the monastic church. Here we had a most delightful dinner in the amazing, vaulted dining room, breakfasted down in the cellars and enjoyed our evening gin and tonic in the monastery's cloister garden.

From the Porto station with all its incredible tiled frescoes we walked down the pedestrianised Rua das Flores to an old palace, now a hotel that was quite delightful. Built on the side of a hill, one was able to go out into the garden from about the third floor, but most surprising was the swimming pool in the cellar which we found to be a Roman bath complete with jacuzzi bubbles at every available seated corner, between square pillars and under blue lighting giving the feel of a blue lagoon, Roman-style.

The Hotel Alfonso XIII in Seville is simply fabulous with a stylish small garden, beautifully furnished public rooms and a selection of Andalusian, Moorish and Castilian bedrooms, our room was so comfortable.

The Sultan owned Al Bustan Palace Hotel was a true experience. In 2006 four of us were visiting Oman and returned to this Muscat Hotel after every sortie be it into the desert, down to Salalah in the south or north to Khasab. Each time our room was of a different style reflecting the Omani culture and traditions. The gardens were superb and the beach wonderful, the pools and even the tennis courts – how could one fail to enjoy?

From that awful no-star hotel on the Nepal Tibet border which one would not recommend one's worst enemy (if one had one!) to the Ritz, what a contrast! I have been most generously invited to stay several times and enjoyed an enormous amount of fun. The staff are incredible, nothing is too much trouble and beyond the area serving the very special teas the hotel soon feels like one's haven. I most certainly cannot say it is 'home from home' – my own home is truly a different size, style and standard not to mention its lack of staff – my home is where catastrophes happen. They most certainly do not at the Ritz, and if they did … well you wouldn't have an inkling!

Chapter 12
Toilets

'Any port in a storm' comes to mind, but when desperate what is there and where are they to be found? Skiing in Europe through the 60s-80s was interesting, yes, the toilets did improve, but life was often a challenge. From the surprise of entering the 'Turkish' toilet cubicle especially when wearing salopettes, or even the 'all in one' ski suit, came only as bad luck. Or the shock at the top of the mountain right on the Austrian/Italian border where waste appeared to go abroad – freezing on the way down the rock face!

Yes, many of us have experienced the complexities of airport toilets, whether one must go through a turnstile, pay an attendant for the pleasure of two sheets of 'ammo' or just be courageous. We were held up at an Ethiopian airport where the heat was terrific, and where I found that a column of tiny coloured beetles were on the march, straight across the floor over the seat and upwards towards the ceiling. Watching other travellers' faces was the best: horror, terror, indignation, fear and pure amusement, I guess it depended on their level of need or desperation!

On safari, returning to our shared tent in the Tanzanian Selous National Park after a splendid dinner we found the most enormous column of soldier ants travelling across our open 'en-suite' at the rear of the sleeping area. At about eight inches wide, coming in from beneath the palm leaf fence, up and over the closed toilet seat down to the bottom of the back fence and then right up it to travel (I

suppose, I didn't go to see!) down the other side back into the bush. A staff member was called who arrived complete with yes, a rifle and simply swished them in all directions with a hand full of palm leaves … heyho. When asked if they would return, he was emphatic this would simply not happen as "they never use the same highway twice"! (The soldiers of army ants are larger than the workers, having much larger mandibles.) Motto: Never forget to take a torch – you never know who may have reached your destination first!

Back in 1980 when my friend Celia and I travelled from Uruguay to Peru by bus it was the norm for a two-hourly call for a 'flower stop'. Rules were made, ladies to the left and men to the right of the bus. The first few 'stops' were most amusing as some of the ladies realized that the wearing of a panty girdle was not appropriate – how we all laughed at their situation!

We have all had to dash urgently to a restaurant or shop *but* when driving across the Tibetan altiplano, the high-altitude arid steppe known as 'The Roof of the World', our bus stopped for us to photograph the extraordinary view; it was a late February day when we were all

dressed in our thickest winter gear against the wind that had nothing to stop it on its way from Northern Siberia, around Everest, to our two small buses. Yes, I thought, the most amazing sight but also a good opportunity for a little relief; no bushy-bushy there, nothing but tiny cairns and tufts of dry grass. So, back behind the bus, down with the 'all-in-one' cosy ski suit, only for our driver to start the engine and drive off. Oh my, a simple case of caught with 'trousers down'! Yes, an adrenalin rush but no great panic as I knew the other bus was miles back and with only one road, zero problem. It was a wind-up (excuse the pun), he drove just a short way and enjoyed the sport!

Speaking of bushy-bushy, when in Venezuela travelling down the Carrao River in a bongo (wooden dug out) we would come off the river at night to hang our hammocks beneath a palm-roofed, open-sided hut. A spade with toilet roll was provided with instructions not to go too far. One returned with

an amused and satisfied face of 'been there, mission accomplished – your turn'. At the end of the journey, finally, we found luxury: a basic toilet block.

Bhutan was truly a bushy-bushy scenario, with a problem that the forest was normally far too dense, so again, it was back behind the bus. With about 17 bends to each kilometre of road there was rarely another vehicle in sight or hearing, but Sod's law does prevail on the odd occasion.

Africa must be the real bushy-bushy but in the Kalahari Desert we spent a night in the Nxai Pan. It is a large salt pan, a topographic depression, which is part of the Makgadikgadi Pans where absolutely nothing lives. We drove, crunching our way across the salt, finally stopping in the middle of 'nowhere', where our guides set out our bed rolls and even a tiny bedside table – exciting. Our

dinner was cooked on the back of the truck – simply wonderful, but not before they had placed a 'thunder box' over a newly dug hole and then put a three-sided tent around it. Our 'room with a view'.

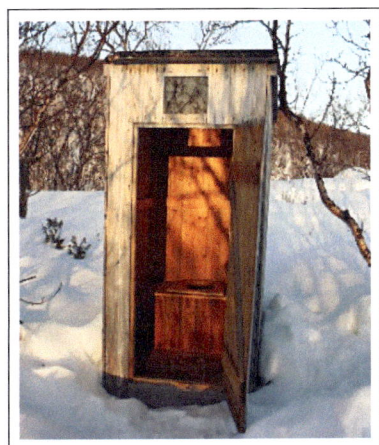

And another 'room with a view' experience was in Finnmark, Norway while on migration with the Sámi and their reindeer herd. Here the seat was surprisingly made of polystyrene for that warm comfort feeling!

Of course, it is only ridiculous situations I write about, but there were other splendours at the other end of the spectrum, such as the famous Japanese toilets, sporting 'all singing and dancing', with heated seats, and a choice of temperature too. Jet spray from beneath or even dare I say – a blow dry! These come with instructions too. Their signs had me in tucks.

Baths and showers also come in every type and 'rating'. Never has a shower tap been the same, the size, the waterpower, the temperature or even the colour. Up the Orinoco we were provided with an old oil drum of river water and a cut-down milk container with which one simply

swished over oneself, letting the water fall back through the slatted floor to the river: a similar container flushed the toilet!

When we arrived at our 'hotel from hell' at Goba, beside the Bale Mountains National Park, Ethiopia, the maid was just going around the perimeter of the rooms and bathroom with petrol (so we were told) to keep away the cockroaches!

On my travels to these remote destinations, the shower doors rarely had a latch. If there was a dry spot or shelf one was lucky; one often had company, be it a spider, frog or gecko on the sill or wall, yes: 'dear diary' and most certainly dinner conversation!

At least the bath I found abandoned on Matya Island, Kuril Islands, Kamchakta, made an unusual place to bird watch!

When in a 'White Van Man's sized campervan' in Tasmania we were travelling from Mount Misery Nature Reserve to Hobart when we came upon a wine and cheese farm. Needless to say, all four of us were up for both the wine and the cheese tastings. Although none of us was keen on the wines, we did find the cheese passable, and we were all most amused when taking advantage of their toilet. There were cartoons all over the walls with reference to sheep. Why do Scotsmen wear a kilt? So the sheep won't hear the zippers! What do you call a sheep without legs? A cloud. How does 'Lamb Chop' get from paddock to paddock? In her Lamborghini! Why did the sheep get arrested? She made a ewe turn! Oh deary me, that is enough!

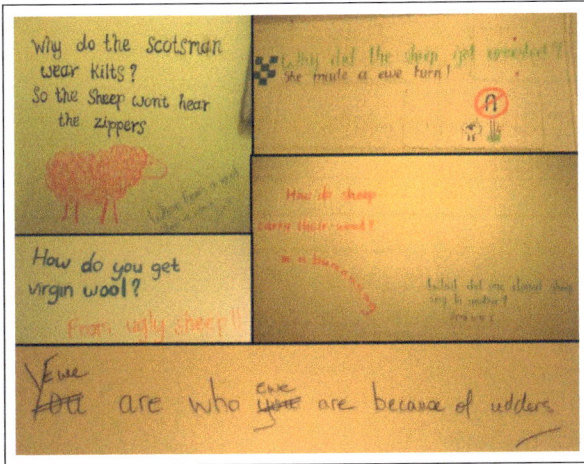

Now, I really don't want to put anyone off travelling but when one comes across some less savoury places just laugh. Ok, I suppose for a chap, but for the ladies the square concrete block about 18 inches high with shaped bowl set within was one such challenge that was offered to us at the beach restaurant on an island off Madagascar; it was most certainly a good

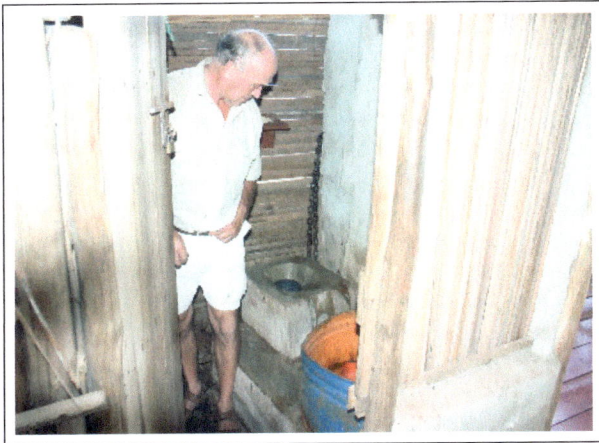

laugh especially when we realised that there was a 'decorative' chain hanging: suddenly we all felt our need evaporating!

And then the ultimate kitsch in a KwaZulu-Natal hotel, where we stopped off for coffee, all it needed was a knitted toilet roll cover!

Upwards and onwards.

Chapter 13
Music

Music across the world is so diverse and yet it is only at times when one sits down to think about the differences does one realise how amazing is the development and variety of the seven continents.

On my first visit to Jersey back in 1953, Coronation year, the local band was parading up the street, with sounds of much umpa-pa! Again, in Buenos Aires 1980 we came across a street parade at the Plaza de Mayo. All the young people and participants were in colourful costumes; there were pipe bands, castanets and shells being played with simply no pushing and shoving at all. Such a joy.

Around the corner we found the amazing sound of the tango, with a couple giving the most wonderful display of this incredible dance. On this visit to Buenos Aires, we took the opportunity to go to the Theatre Colon for a performance of Schumann's *Scenes from Faust* with the Philharmonic Orchestra and the Wagner Singers. The next two visits to Buenos Aires, the theatre was under renovations but finally on my last visit I was able to see all the magnificent work they had done, but sadly I was not there long enough to enjoy a further concert! Travelling across

the country, we encountered the panpipes which come in so many sizes. To sit outside with a cool drink and listen to these sounds is near to heaven!

Needless to say, crossing this great continent we visited many churches, both urban and extremely rural. Each had an organ of scale according to the building, so many times we were able to sit and listen to these glorious sounds, sometimes with magnificent acoustics. More often though, I hasten to add, it was a comfort to simply sit for the relative cool or warmth – naughty!

Colombia is another most colourful country; I was introduced to Angela, the owner and organiser of the 'Delirio Hecho en Cali', at a private party and then later met Leanora and Andrea who had started it, along with Angela 10 years previously. Luckily for us, on our return to Cali there was one of the monthly performances and we were invited. These are unique, being salsa dancing of all types and so much more besides. Initially the entrance is a malaise of performers, trapeze, stalls or various whisky stands, performing photos and giveaways. Arriving in the

auditorium, we had a brilliant table with an excellent view of the stage. The performances included some acrobatics, very loud South American music and of course much Salsa. An incredible evening even if it took me several days to get my ears back to 100% working order!

Another Colombian party with fabulous music was the band at Patricia's

70th birthday party. Her whole family were fantastic singers also and were very quick to join the band, taking the microphone and giving everyone much entertainment.

Totally different are the 'throat singers' I have listened

to, an amazing feat of breathing control. My first encounter was in Shingkar, eastern Bhutan when staying at a farmhouse way up in the woodlands (yeti

country). The village ladies came up to join us after dinner and having shown us the traditional Bhutanese dances we were invited to join too. Two of the ladies started to sing this incredible method of question and answer singing. Again, in Norway, with the Sámi, I came across their singing known as the 'joik' but it was not until I reached Eclipse Sound, Pond Inlet up on the eastern side of the Northwest Passage did I hear similar sounds again of those Bhutanese ladies. An absolute thrill and I remain in awe of their ability.

The Mongolians also have their own style too along with some unique instruments. We were able to acquire

tickets to the Tumen Ekh song and dance ensemble, they played traditional instruments with full scale orchestral renditions of new and old Mongolian music. The outstanding examples of their throat singing, known as 'khoomi' was

totally fascinating. We also enjoyed contortionists who made our eyes water, traditional and modern dancing, plus a recital featuring the unique horse-head violin: called the morin khuur. Finally, there were clowns and festival masked dancers which were very similar to the Bhutanese festivals.

I have been very lucky to have been to Bhutan numerous times, first on the ballooning trip and thereafter either in spring to see all the amazing wild flora and fauna and again in the autumn when clear skies with glorious

mountain views are more frequent, but of course the landscape is not so colourful. However the locals are always willing to join us with music and dance.

My first visit was in November 1998, for this was when the weather was to be the most suitable for ballooning. So enamoured was I at the beauty of the country that I was determined to return in springtime. This chance came in 2001 when Jude and I travelled to Delhi to do a round trip of the 'triangle' before flying into Paro, Bhutan's only airport at that time, to meet another friend at the airport.

On this trip we joined the Ura Festival, usually known as the Yak Festival as our visit coincided with the Yak farmers' celebrations before going up into the mountains with the herds for the summer. On the first evening the festival began in the monastery followed by a visit to the grounds for blessings. Many carried flame sticks, the drums and cymbals were played as the prayers were said along with the sounds of conch shells and of course the enormous horns.

The following morning more of the yak herders had assembled and were ready to enjoy all the traditional dances including the Shacham, the Dance of the Four Stags. As always, the dancing stags were wearing knee-length brightly coloured yellow silk skirts with masks of horned deer. Each of the numerous dances at the festivals have a long history from the introductory sheet given to us on the day, this particular one originated when: "Ugyen Rinpoche was in the world; he subdued the King of the Wind who created much unhappiness through his great power by making all sentient beings and the world tremble. Ugyen Rinpoche rode the stag when he subdued the earth and appeased all beings by establishing peace and happiness. As a blessing the first incarnation of Nam Nying (Namkhe Nyingpo) found the effigy of a face of a stag and hence the dance of the white stag came to be. During this dance the gratitude of the pious people is demonstrated to all the beings destined to be converted in the future. After all the agitation of the world have been overcome, happiness and peace will reign supreme."

I always loved the Black Hat Dance (Shana), mostly because of the amazing costumes: a large black hat, felt boots, colourful brocade with a long gown but in this case, no mask! The Black Neck Crane Festival at Gangtey was unique and delightful, we were so lucky to be there in 2008 for that wonderful occasion. Earlier in the morning we had walked across the frosty moor to see

the rare cranes who fly across the Himalayas to winter in Gangtey. On the same trip we also visited the Jambay Lhakhang field in Jakar for the Fire Blessing Festival. Oh my, this was at night, so dark was it but for the arch of flames that the brave of us had to walk through for our 'fire blessing' and to be purified!

I took a party of 12 on that trip, a few weeks before we were to leave home, we learned that we had struck gold in as much as the 4th King of Bhutan had abdicated in favour of his son and the dates that we were due to be in Thimphu were chosen for the 5th King's coronation.

We were uncertain what this would entail, but my, we were given the opportunities to be involved in the most unique occasions that unfolded before our very eyes.

On the day, November 6th, 2008, we went to the Palace, we could see the giant sacred Thongdrels (tapestries) hanging on the side of the Dzong where inside the religious coronation service was proceeding. We then went down to the area where the King would receive his people who, as always, would offer him a white silk scarf – we had ours and had learned and practised the traditional method of offering. Sadly, the organisation went wrong, and the flow of the people came to naught but throughout this part of the festival we could hear the sound of the drums, cymbals and horns.

The new King was so upset that he couldn't meet his people that he promised to have yet another day in the stadium where he could right this error.

The following day my group were to climb up to Taktshang Goemba (Tiger's Nest) but a friend and I chose to return to Thimphu to hopefully see the King within the stadium where his people would give their offering. As we neared the capital the crowds were gathering, walking from far and wide to be there within the brand-new stadium. There were elephants walking into town and other strange animals who, we would learn,

were traditional offerings from different districts to the King. I was dressed in my Bhutanese clothes and was accompanied by the young cousin of Tashi, who I had met in 2001 when he was our guide.

This time Tashi was responsible for the security of the King's VVIP, Sonia Ghandi, he also trained the troops for the Grand Parade. To the minute, the music started and the King arrived, followed by the chief Llama, VVIPs, VIPs and the rest of the entourage. Tensing (known as 'Mike'), Tashi's friend through college carried the national flag while Tashi led the parade. After the Military Parade, there was music, dancing and further parades but at around midday the 5th King came into the stand to meet his people. He sat amongst them chatting and enjoying their company, it brought tears to one's eyes to see the love between them all. Amazingly, he came along to where we were to chat. Again, he was so warm and easy to speak with, it seemed completely natural. He made us laugh so much.

When he asked where I came from, I said that I lived north of Oxford just off the M40 knowing that he had been to university there. He was very quick with a quip regarding the difference between Cambridge and Oxford

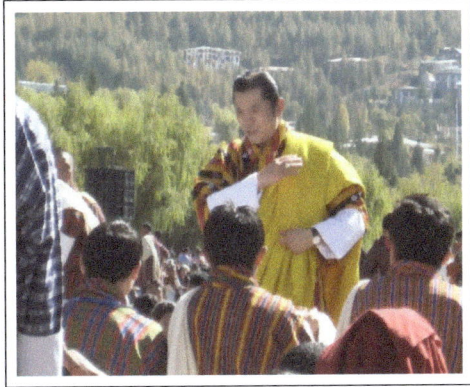

Universities after an American lady behind me commented that she had been at Cambridge.

The following day, Tashi invited me to sit in one of the VIP tents for the extra day's celebrations. This event was organised at the very last minute because of the problems of the 5th King's people not being able to meet him personally on Coronation Day. What a success that day was. The whole of the centre of the stadium as well as the stands were filled with orderly, almost silent families. Rows and rows sat quietly across this great sward awaiting the King who bent at 90 degrees to greet each person individually. Periodically he would join the dancing simply to give himself a chance to stand upright and enjoy the camaraderie.

Learning of the unprecedented turn out of people, more and more of the royal family joined him. Again, along he came to our tent and greeted us with such graciousness even asking us quite unnecessarily if we had anything to

eat. We assured him that we were provided for, and were happy, and offered him some Walker's shortbread, which we happened to have with us. He was overjoyed and immediately put it safely into his Gho (Bhutanese national dress for men).

Later, his brother the Prince came along offering us the national gifts that we had already received from the King. He too was most gracious and again enquired if we were comfortable and had eaten; impressed too that we said that we had already received the gifts. An amazing day to have experienced indeed. That day I wasn't in my Kira, the Bhutanese national dress, and sadly didn't join in as I am not very proficient at their dances. The music however was wonderful. I was happy to watch all the various styles from across the numerous districts – all so diverse.

There are many tsechus across the country at various times of the year, each unique and well supported as blessings are gained for participation.

When we found ourselves at the Tiger Festival in southern India in 1991 the music sounded cacophonous to our ears. Alive, crowded, colourful, loud and disorganised as far as one could see, but the theme was celebrating the Tiger and the goddess, Mariyamma, at the Mariyamma Temple built 800 years ago which is five kilometres from the Mangaladevi Temple where her sister is. We met the Goddess Mariyamma being carried aloft when we returned from visiting her sister after which we were invited to go into the temple for a blessing. All around us there were many who had gone into a trance and had to be carried away; others were deep breathing and crying out, 'performing' right beside us. Apparently, the goddess lands on them and off into their 'other world' they go.

I hoped that she wouldn't land on me; Anil, one of our guides was extremely frightened but our courier was laughing which was when three of us went in to be 'blessed'. All the others of our group were far too scared. That was some experience, I must confess. Meanwhile the dancing continued, with firecrackers, gambling, games, stalls and even a 'wooden Ferris wheel' that was being driven by some local lads within it, climbing from 'spoke to spoke' – braking similarly too. A sight I shall never forget – health and safety certainly not on anyone's agenda there! Apparently between 20,000 and 40,000 people regularly came to this festival. Yes, it was crowded that is for sure.

While travelling along the Blue Ridge Mountains of Virginia we were advised that the musical evening at the Floyd County Store was something that should not be missed. We knew little of what we were to encounter except that many Mennonites and groups who wear their traditional clothes frequented the town.

We were there at the store in very good time, finding ourselves first in the queue for the office to open at 4.45pm. We were joined by large numbers

of locals of many trades and religious groups – it was a delight to chat to them. We were thrilled to be able to gain seats in the second row – the front row being reserved for the regulars. Having left our coats upon our chosen chairs we went up the street to Oddfella's Cantina, a very good name for a way-out food house. We had such fun!

But back to take up our seats and for the music. We were not disappointed. A major part of the shop had been cleared of the retail stands and rails – all wheeled away. The band was setting up on the stage and the

145

folk were turning up in great numbers. Happily for us, some locals failed to turn up and we were invited into the front row, straight onto the dance floor!

The Reverend, whether local resident or a visitor I do not know, started the evening with prayers followed by Janet Turner and friends who proceeded to give us their local Blue Grass music for a good hour. The songs were very bible orientated: "Lord, give us a ladder to Heaven, but we are not ready to go quite yet", etc. She had a double bass player and a guitarist; they were both most amusing; she must have been the wrong side of 70 but most certainly a game old bird! From then on, it was go, go, go as Janet came to an end, we could see the locals waxing their dancing shoes, shuffling in their seats to be ready to take to the floor.

Much amused by this and chatting to the 'regular' couple sitting next to me I was keen to take part also. So off with my shoes (non-slippery), with socks well waxed, away we went straight onto the floor to perform our own form of the soft-shoe shuffle, dancing amongst the professional regulars was nothing but hilarious. We mixed amongst those who were good, very good as well as simply hopeless – it mattered not: young, old and just like us – not caring one iota but laughing at ourselves all the way. We had a ball!

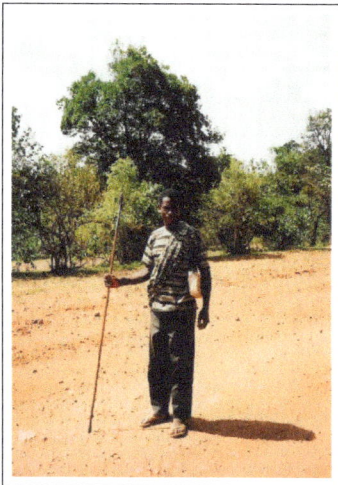

Ethiopia most certainly had musicians, they could be seen in the street, and out in the countryside but the one that made me smile the most was the 'farmer' who I spotted with both spear and transistor – an incongruous sight! So widely is music appreciated across the globe.

Chapter 14
Hospitals

I have always been interested to see how other countries handle the medical and education strategies with their diverse economic situations.

When visiting Malawi with a medical friend we stayed near the Queen Elizabeth Hospital in Blantyre where she was able to give a lecture to the doctors and senior staff, during which I was given a tour of some of the children's wards. Their lack of equipment was there before my very eyes. A child was lying on what looked like a large wooden tray, but was his bed; he lay there quietly with a rope around his ankle and a brick tied to it hanging over the end. He had a broken leg and this method was to aid the bone to knit correctly. This 'bed' was cheek by jowl with many other orthopaedic cases. Outside on the hillside beside the institution the patients' families were camping and cooking to provide food as this was not provided by the hospital at all; some had walked miles to bring the patients to the hospital.

The sight of some of these poor little imps was heartrending, but the hospital staff were doing the best that they could with the basic facilities they had. Out in the countryside, there were clinics where the medical staff would travel to on a regular basis – quite how often this was, depended on availability and accessibility.

Returning from Bhutan Spring 2007, we stayed in Calcutta giving us time to visit the Mother Teresa Sanctuary. Our first stop was her 'Home for the Dying' which was situated near the Kali Temple, the most important

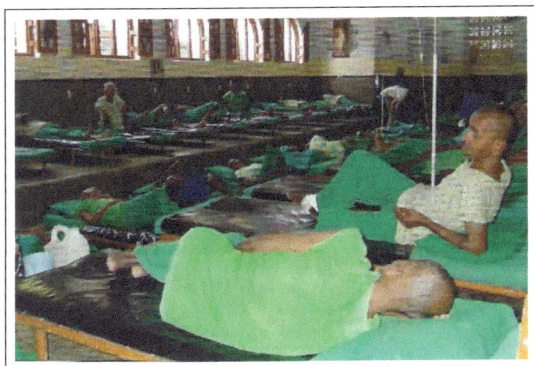

place in the city. From our bus, we walked down the road where there were lots of beggars and street sellers around and generally people living out their lives on the street – very colourful and so different to our culture.

We stepped off the noisy, bustling street into a hallway of calm, quiet and serenity before stepping immediately into the men's ward which was indeed quite a shock. There were rows of basic wooden beds with the patients lying or sitting. A few of us walked amongst them, some put their hands together in prayer – one could only do the same and even clasp them giving warmth and comfort; this was the universal language of communication.

While we were still visiting an Italian lady came with baskets of food. She was an important businesswoman who had felt the call to help and came to her Calcutta apartment for six months of each year. I went on into the women's ward and then into the sluicing room and mortuary, the latter a grim reminder of the purpose of this whole 'sanctuary'; it was so wonderful to see the marvellous work being so quietly attended to by the nuns and volunteers.

We continued upstairs to the chapel where a couple of us joined the nuns in their Easter Week service. The whole area was therefore decorated for the religious festival with a banner showing Jesus surrounded by blue and white dressed nuns of the Sisters of Charity. We were then able to visit Mother Teresa's grave, there beside the chapel.

We then drove on to the Children's Home of the Sisters of Charity. We were invited into the ward with both mentally and physically handicapped children; some of these little mites were sadly very sick indeed.

For me, the next experience was the hardest – we went out into the garden to visit the children playing. They looked well and happy, mostly abandoned and apparently could be adopted. The eldest was probably about eight; they go to school from the centre. But although some were shy, others would come and latch on to us like limpets wanting, quite rightly, love and affection. But trying to get away to leave was both heartrending and physically quite difficult.

On another trip to Bhutan, I was invited to visit the main hospital in Thimphu. Relative to Malawi, a very much more modern and attractive building with marvellous facilities. Bhutan's education and medical services are free. Many foreign countries have helped finance this emerging enclave which is super organised and very forward thinking in its attitude to its people. We were able to visit the ICU, the maternity and orthopaedic wards.

We could see the outpatients too, where everyone was calm. Hospital life seemed very well run indeed.

During one trip to Bhutan, one of our party was feeling very poorly; happily one of the group was a medic and knew exactly what she needed. Just a phone call to the tiny hospital along our route enabled us to call in, see the resident doctor and receive the remedy with tremendous kindness.

On that same trip our guide again called ahead to see if we could visit the boarding school for blind children. There were albinos as well as the partially and fully blind youngsters who all seemed extremely happy, learning crafts as well as being educated. This was again an insight into the help and guidance being provided for these unfortunate Bhutanese. We watched them with their one-to-one education which included braille. They were all so pleased to receive us and within minutes a mini concert was organised in their multi-purpose hall (gym, chapel, music room). Eight children supported by a Yamaha keyboard and a Yengchin, which one of our party said was similar to a Hungarian zither that has knobs and is struck by a bamboo wand. We all enjoyed the musical event thoroughly.

In Ethiopia, I came across a group of young volunteer opticians who had gone out to help with a mobile eye clinic. A couple of them would go ahead to organise the village venue, providing posters with the day they were coming and inviting the locals to attend. Then the next group would arrive with all the testing kit, spare glasses that could be handed out and any medication that may be required. As we drove through one village, we saw this in action – these volunteers certainly were doing an excellent and much needed service.

I was both honoured and most appreciative of being invited to visit 'The Club Noel' hospital for poor children in Cali, Colombia November 2016. This

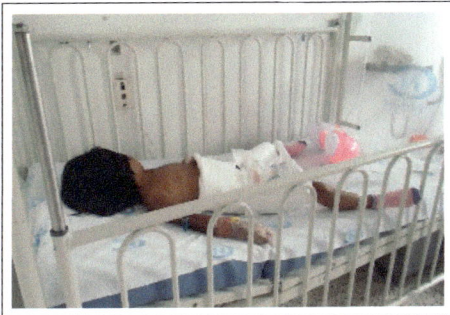

is a privately financed hospital for the poorest of the city. Twenty thousand children were being seen each month; it was the most incredible place. There were day patients, an A & E wing, long-term and even an intensive care

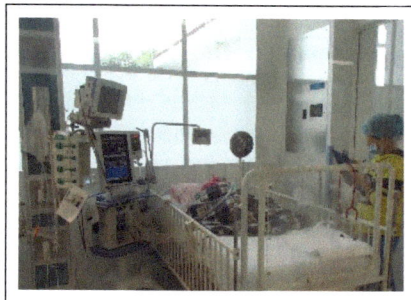

wing which had 20 beds each with individual equipment. There were operating rooms, X-ray and scanning sections, all with the best equipment possible. We were taken around many of the wards and waiting rooms; their next hope was for an oncology wing. I was privileged to meet specialists, doctors, nurses, volunteers and medical students too. Princess Anne had visited in 2007 when she had spent two hours walking round and was apparently most impressed as indeed, was I. It was most uplifting to see the love, care, cleanliness, tranquility and organisation given to these little mites.

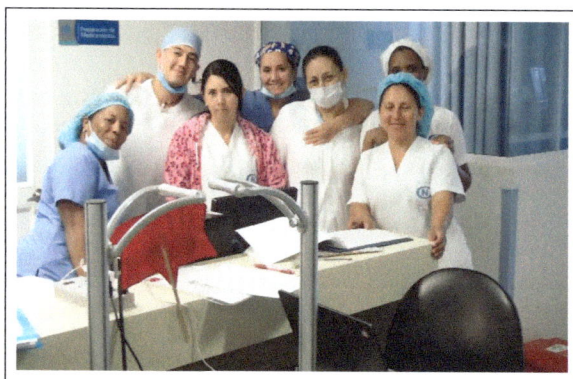

That same day we also visited the 'home' called 'Casita de Belen' for abandoned children. Again, this is a most wonderful institution with about 80 babies and children living there plus a further 250 visiting daily. We saw the tiniest sitting quietly in a row of rockers, these had arrived in recent days found on doorsteps, in the street or even left at 'Casita de Belen's' door. There were others being fed in highchairs while others played in a large playpen. We visited their dormitories, one for the boys and

another for the girls each filled with cots and beds, a play area and yet another room with a television and writing area.

There was a large and a small play area, numerous classrooms and of course the dining area which was very busy while we were there with the

little ones enjoying their lunch. The kitchen was good, the stores and even the laundry excellent, each child having its own individually marked clothes.

We were taken to the IT room where the older of the children were learning computer studies; this was next door to the storeroom that held the gifts that had come in from factories, businesses and private donations: clothes, toys, shoes, furniture etc. There was a clinic and sanatorium – all this work is

so worthwhile. Run by Gloria, who is so dedicated, she works there every weekday for no payment at all. Again, having been into the playground with the youngsters, it was hard to get away. Well done to all who work in these wonderful sanctuaries.

From the charity run hospitals we needed an unscheduled visit to A & E on our way back from Mount Tamborine near Coolangatta, Australia December 2012. Our hiking leader had stepped on a branch that had swung up and hit her shin, cutting it badly. She being a medic had looked after it over the weekend but felt it needed further attention, so on our way home we called in at the hospital. This was both an education as well as being entertaining especially with the memories of my previous foreign hospital visits in mind; Mich had to check in explaining her problem at a 'bank' style counter (remember those?), then on to the next counter to pay or show her health card (no National Health in Australia). We then sat, sat and sat for 90 minutes after which she went up to say, "How much longer?" – immediately she was through, given a bed and 20 minutes later a Scottish nurse dressed the leg and off home we went. But while we waited, we watched, with silent amazement, all the folk coming in with their various problems: dog bites, swollen lip, gammy legs, and others who we would never know their reason for coming.

All this is a world away from the dentistry I saw out in the street around the Barkhor in Lhasa in 1987. Open-pedal cranked machines running like bicycle chains driving drills to do their evil deed! I cringe now even thinking about what I saw alongside those dentists; the butchers table, the air blue with

flies, vegetables all just above the open drain/sewer. Dear diary, memories indeed! There were some things in those days one didn't photograph but the people were often very happy indeed to share the moment.

Chapter 15
Some Special Species Seen

I am always willing to clamber through the jungle, work my way through bushes, hike over hillsides, struggle across the snow or even take to the water to seek out a sighting of one of the world's rare or endangered creatures. Madagascar was such an island where four of us spent a month searching out endemic creatures. Lemurs, birds, frogs, chameleons, insects, butterflies, the fossa and much more. Many times, with our specialist

Fossa

local guides we would cut our way through thick undergrowth to get the slightest sighting or, better still a picture, as not all these creatures are generous enough to hang around for long. Often, we did have results from our hard work which is so satisfying. In the evenings

Coquerel's coua

instead of relaxing, socialising and discussing the day's sightings we would be whisked off forevermore, once again trundling through narrow paths back into the bush to find the nocturnal creatures. It was not until then

Night lemur

Chameleon

that we all appreciated the quantity of activity there is out there. To search for and find the night lemurs, frogs, chameleons, moths, fireflies, and spiders, to enjoy the scents and sounds was all such an exciting experience, even if the ants did find a way beneath my trousers or a leach clasp itself to my chin along the way! We had timed this trip to coincide with the mating season of the fossa (a cat-like, carnivorous mammal endemic to Madagascar). Sadly, we missed that activity by a couple of weeks (global warming?) but we did see just one in the end. We were thrilled to have a sighting also of a black parrot (the greater vasa parrot) and at another time, the Coquerel's coua. I

was most interested in the pachypodiums (elephant's foot plants) we found across the barren plain of the Canyon des Singes but the spiny forest is unique, extraordinary and fabulous, and undoubtedly peculiar to Madagascar. This forest extends from

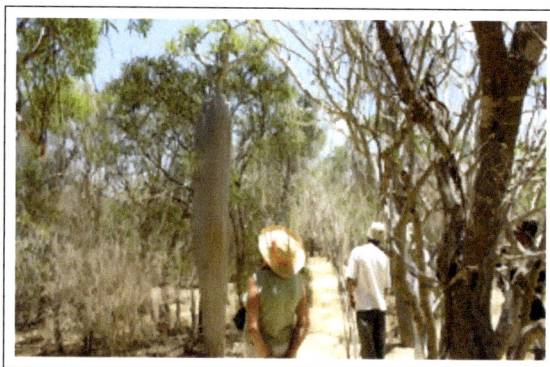

Morombe in the southwest right around the southern coast and almost as far as Fort-Dauphin and some 50km inland. The vegetation comprises a type of deciduous thicket or thorn scrub, dominated by members of the didiereaceae family and species of euphorbia. They grow in all shapes and sizes with few leaves to transpire, some with enormous spines to deter birds and animals from stealing any precious water they may be storing, as they sometimes must last up to a year without. We found different pachypoda, tree euphorbia and various types of baobabs as well as many rare endemic birds including

154

the long-tailed ground roller (the only one with a long tail), the subdesert mesite with its long and downward-curved bill, a sickle-billed vanga, Archbold's newtonia, subdesert brush warbler, the running coua, a Madagascar plover and some beautifully made nests especially the paradise fly catcher. All on one unbelievable hike, but that beer I can tell you after such an arid morning's activity was more than welcome!

Paradise fly catcher

Africa, like South America, has such diverse conditions with many species of flora and fauna restricted to very small areas. In Ethiopia I was over the moon to find 11 Simien wolves,

Ethiopian wolf / Simien fox / Simien jackal

Africa's most endangered canid one of a group who are highly specialised feeders eating only Afro-alpine rodents such as giant mole-rats of which there were many darting about. Up there on the top of the Sanetti Plateau in the Bale Mountains we also found blue-winged geese,

just one Abyssinian hare and a couple of klipspringers. Walking amongst an enormous troop of gelada monkeys was very special. These are also only found in the Ethiopian Highlands foraging on the grasslands. The plants, too, were simply incredible, including tree heath, giant lobelia, yellow

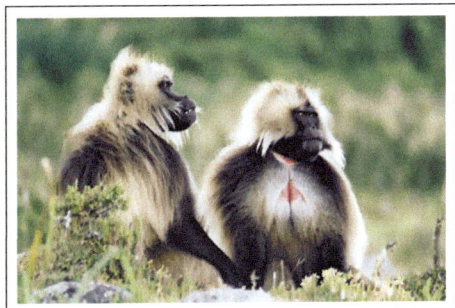

Gelada monkeys

155

primrose, gentians, plus lush mosses and lichens that hung from the trees.

Sadly, our guide named the many birds far too quickly for me to note their species, for we saw so many. In the Negele district I was able to go walking, to find the Negele lark, the Degodi lark along with vultures, grasshoppers buzzards, buff-breasted and white-bellied bustards, Somali bee-eaters, black-throated barbets, red-naped bush-shrikes, rufous-tailed rock-thrushs, short-billed crombecs, Somali tits, straw-tailed wydahs and buntings – a good few days!

We also visited the Sof Omar cave, claimed to be the longest system of caves in Africa. Although not a great lover of caves, but falling as always for a challenge, I scrambled down to see the thousands of bats hanging from above. As there were many insects the swifts and swallows were busy in a feeding frenzy. There were some fish in the water that I couldn't identify but I was pleased to know that the crocodiles that live in the nearby river did not frequent that dark cave!

It is said that to spend time with the gorillas is life changing and they most certainly are wonderful creatures. I was so happy to be able to sit for an hour with a troupe in Uganda and again in Rwanda. It was very hard work climbing up the side of the volcano but that matters little once you are in their company.

Gorilla

Tree lion

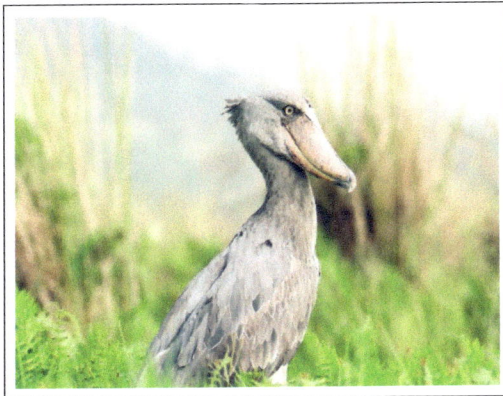

Shoebill

The tree lions of Queen Elizabeth Park in Uganda were so funny, lounging about up the trees like leopards – their aroma comes with them, that is for sure! I was surprised how large the chimpanzees were that we also found in the park, they were most certainly extremely strong.

Whilst in Rwanda I was very pleased to go off very early one morning in search of the shoebill. My boatman paddled the two of us through the reeds, papyrus and other water plants until he finally spotted one for me. They are so prehistoric looking.

The wildlife of southern Africa is also tremendous. My first sighting of an elephant was way back in 1975 when taken to Wankie Game Reserve, Rhodesia since then I have seen many but none so amazing as those down by the Chobe River in Botswana. Out of all the predators seen on safari; the lions, leopards and cheetahs, the latter is my favourite. But sitting in a safari vehicle, as I have been twice surrounded by a pack of wild dogs, is totally breathtaking.

The different species of antelope are not always easy to identify. I have been so lucky to see the sitatunga

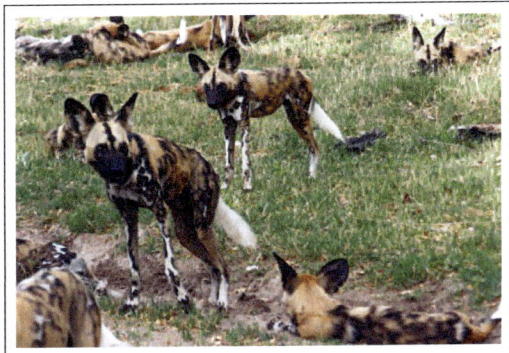

Wild dogs

157

racing through the water bodies, the puku too and my favourite the sable. Never am I happier than out on safari, whatever the weather, looking for that flick of a tail, twitch of an ear, the great curl of the greater kudu's horn or enormous eland. The rhino is so special, I have

Leopard

'enjoyed' a roadblock of three adults halting my progress through a park in KwaZulu-Natal. I have sadly encountered poaching a couple of times too, in Hluhluwe National Park and in Thula Thula. Unforgivable.

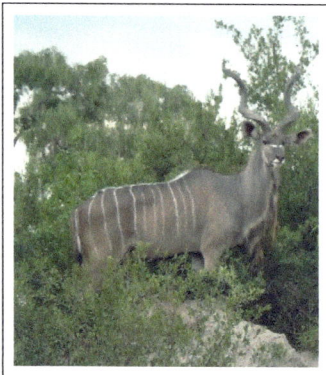

Kudu

The elephants at the Thula Thula reserve are most special, having been saved by Lawrence Anthony from being put down, they have settled there and are now breeding successfully. Their story is told in his book *The Elephant Whisperer* which brings tears to one's eyes. More tears came to my eyes when

I watched the zebra and wildebeest on migration. The sounds of the stallion zebra calling his mares, and these in turn keeping an eye on their foals when the snorts of the wildebeest

Zebra and Wildebeest

continued as they passed by can only be described as spine-tingling.

Waiting crocodiles are a tour de force, but I always try to help my feelings by telling myself that they can only catch one at a time! When visiting the

Mongooses and Boomslang

information centre in the Serengeti we were greeted by the fascinating sight of a troop of tame hyrax lying all over the rocks sunning themselves. Beside them was a group of mongooses surrounding and teasing a huge eastern green mamba (later confirmed as a boomslang). This snake had blown out its neck and looked like a cobra. I later learned it is most unusual to find them on the ground, for boom means tree in Afrikaans, and they normally inhabit trees where they feed on birds' eggs.

Experiencing a hot air balloon flight was great fun, enjoying the special sights of the oxbow lakes, formed by the meandering rivers below and the yellow-billed storks nesting in the treetops. We, the eight 'Migration girls', were very content when our pilot finally made a controlled and safe landing but in a horizontal position. Once the group of giggling females had been helped out and onto their feet to

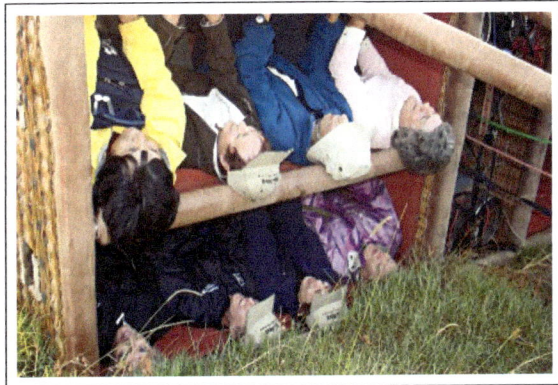

Migration girls

enjoy a glass of champagne followed by a sit-down breakfast, we felt that we richly deserved our certificates. We left the site with another driver, cheering 'African Python' towards our flight pilot finding relief in the absence of suitable bushy-bushy cover!

There have been so many plants and birds in these amazing places it would take a further book to tell the tales of all my sightings, but the paradise

159

whydah I encountered in the Drakensberg left me in wonderment. When we saw them there must have been about 20 flying across the grasslands with their swooping movement. Again, the girls had a job to move me along, when years later, I sighted a tropicbird. I just love them and was overjoyed to spot a breeding pair on a beach in the Seychelles.

The tortoises of the Seychelles islands were also a revelation to me, Many of the tortoises were enclosed in unsavoury pens, and I did wish that they were roaming free. The fish and plants of the island were fantastic especially when we managed to find the great Coco de Mer Forest, where we saw that great seed. We also, luckily, spotted the Seychelles black parrot just beside our bus stop!

Determined to find orangutans on a visit to

Whydah

Tropicbird

Proboscis monkey

Orangutan

Sabah, Borneo, we were not disappointed. We discovered them high in the trees in the wild as well as seeing many when visiting the Sepilok Sanctuary. Proboscis monkeys were also found when we took a boat up the river deep into the forest, what extraordinary creatures they are; a bonus up there was to discover long-tailed macaques too. The flora of the whole area was vibrant and lush, so too the colour and size of so many butterflies.

Our guide was hoping that we would get the chance to see a Rafflesia in flower, though none had been seen for several weeks but happily

as we came away from the natural hot baths there was a sign to say that one was in flower. To see just one of these enormous parasitic flowers, with its incredible buds, was a true experience as they are deemed to be the largest flower in the world.

I was persuaded to go into the Germanton Caves that are renowned for their

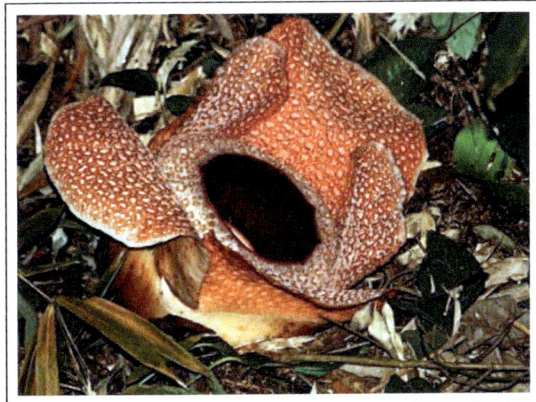

Rafflesia

valued edible swiftlet nests, which are harvested for bird's nest soup. The most valuable of the nests, the white ones, can sell for very high prices. A few licensed locals are traditionally allowed to harvest them twice a year using only rattan ladders, ropes and bamboo poles. As we walked along

Swiftlet cave

the boardwalk with thick guano underfoot as well as on the handrail, the smell was dire, the cockroaches teemed, and a large colony of the wrinkle-lipped free-tailed bats hung from above. Outside we found the bat hawks waiting in the dense forest, never far from the mouth of the cave waiting patiently to prey on the bats as they leave their roost.

The joy when visiting Pulau, Sandakan was collecting eggs from the laying green and hawksbill turtles to bury them at the turtle sanctuary for safety and to return the ones that hatched that evening to the shoreline. Such a privilege.

Turtle sanctuary

Turtle hatchlings

I was very excited to see a sloth bear in Sri Lanka. I had never heard of one before but learning on our first evening at the Yala Park that another vehicle had seen one, I was determined to track

Sloth Bear

162

this creature down. Our driver, 'Chandelier' as we called him, knew where to try to find one so having already found leopards we went off on the most successful mission. It is such a thrill to learn which tracks one is looking for, to find them and then actually succeed.

Up in the Himalayan Kingdom of Bhutan I was also able to enjoy a sighting of their national animal the takin, such a strange looking creature, and also their golden langurs, a black and white squirrel and red pandas. I failed miserably to meet a Yeti but did succeed in sighting the fresh

Takin

footprints of a snow leopard! Leaving Bhutan from the southeast at Samdrup Jongkhar we entered the Kaziranga National Park, Assam where, from the back of an elephant, I encountered numerous Indian rhinoceros quite closely. Since my visit there have been enormous floods where many were lost, and human encroachment to their habitat is a further sadness to their survival.

String of Mongolian horses

On our visit to Outer Mongolia our first Ger Camp was at Erdene Ukhaa which is not far from Mandalgobi but miles from anywhere as far as I was concerned. Our party of four went off on a walk down towards a small lake. The wildflowers and grasses were all out in

163

full flower, their seasons so short like those up in the Arctic regions, where we found tiny 'hamsters' running about. Their true name I never discovered but returning to our ger, I found my brown sandals were totally yellow, covered in the pollen from all those glorious flowers. Across much of the steppe there was a pale purple sheen, this I discovered was from a six-inch allium. We also sighted their two-humped Bactrian camels, ibex, peregrine falcons, rock-thrushes, chats, and many raptors including the greater spotted eagle, black kites and

Bactrian camels

even a pair of lammergeyers beside their nest. The expanse of the countryside is breathtaking, much enhanced by flocks of sheep and goats as well as strings of horses in magnificent condition. The Przewalski horses of Mongolia became extinct in the wild in the late 1960s; from a wild mare introduced into the Ukrainian captive population and the breeding of a few in breeding centres and zoos, a good number have been reintroduced into the wild. We visited the Hustai Nuruu National Park where they have had great success.

Australia and New Zealand have such unique creatures, none more so than what is termed as the 'world's happiest animal' the quokka. These marsupials were found on their home ground of Rottnest Island off Fremantle, wandering around everywhere, either quite oblivious to the humans or simply just used to having so many visitors about during the day. We were guided to an osprey nest that was 60 years old, phenomenal.

Quokka

Echidna

The extraordinary Echidna is one of Australia's strange creatures, I spotted one at the base of a tree beside the road. I hoped it would not go the way of so many of our hedgehogs who are more often seen flat on the road. Alongside the endemic fauna kangaroo, koala and wallaby, we successfully found many highly colourful birds including parrots. My favourite of all is the bellbird with it's marvellous ting-ting chiming sound. When up in the Daintree National Park at Cape Tribulation we went in search of the crocodiles and cassowaries, failing with both but also sadly realising that I was being bitten badly by the sand flies, known there as 'no see ums' – I had failed to spot those blighters too!

Koala

Kookaburra

Galah cockatoo

165

Cane toads are not handsome creatures; they were surrounding the swimming pool at our campsite near Burrum Heads along with an enormous, injured iguana, but the lovely flying possums were a delight. On our daily walks around the Gold Coast there were many black swans, Baillon's crake, Pacific black duck, Pacific baza, pied butcherbirds, kerrawang and of course the kookaburra. Up in the Lamington National Park, sadly seriously burnt through during the fires of 2019/2020, I was lucky to see endless 'new to me' birds as we trundled through that wonderful forest. Brushturkey, crimson rosella, king parrot, eastern spinebill, satin bowerbird, grey and rufous fantails, the amazing eastern whipbird, eastern yellow robin, red-browed finch, wonga pigeon, white-browed scrubwren, yellow-throated scrubwren, Lewin's honeyeater and the welcome swallow. The red-necked pademelon even came

Red-necked pademelon

to join us at our tent. It was such an asset to have a real birder with us, a girl who knows all the plants as well and had the energy and enthusiasm to keep us going for weeks.

Visiting my friends farm near Gunnedah we found ever more birds and animals including galahs, sulphur-crested cockatoos, spotted harrier, swamp wallabies, wallaroos, agile wallabies, white and yellow-tailed black cockatoos, red-tailed black cockatoos, diamond firetail, mistletoebird, white-eared honeyeater, eastern honeyeater and even the blue-tongued skink. The wildlife sanctuary in the town of Gunnedah had many birds and animals that were in varying stages of health, having

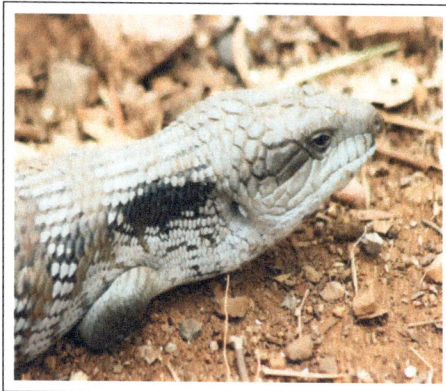

Blue-tongued skink

166

been brought in after accidents or tragedy. One large ostrich was in full male muster with his bright red legs and took a shine to me, apparently it was something to do with the colours I was wearing – he started to do his mating dance, which kept us all much amused. He

Ostrich

bent right back on his heels whilst swinging his body and neck in rhythm left and right and as I walked up or down the wire he followed me in dire earnest! Motto: if you wish this attention, wear your safari colours!

In Tasmania we passed through the village of Doo where every house appeared to have a name which includes the word Doo, near there at an isthmus known as 'The Neck' we discovered an eastern blue-tongue skink and later a pair of Bennett's wallaroos. Further on at Bicheno we found the fairy penguins. It was such fun waiting for them to gather into a raft for safety and then rush out of the water together to waddle as fast as they could across the beach up to their burrows in the bushes. Near Cradle Mountain at our Discovery Park

Bennett's wallaroos (red-necked wallabies)

Camp, I was so lucky to see a wombat before it scuttled back into the woodland, I never saw another but on the same walk I did see my first blonde kangaroo.

Blonde kangaroo

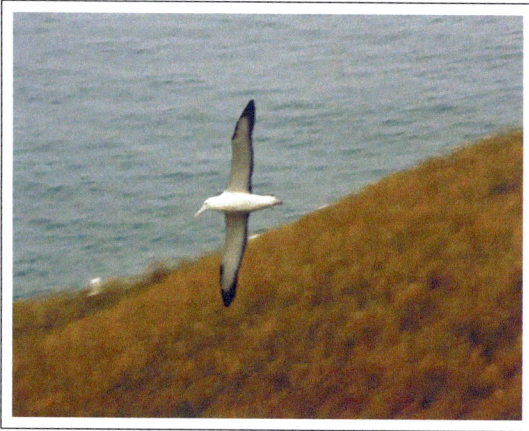

Royal albatross

The royal albatross soaring in the sky on their huge wings and nesting on the hillside was a joy. On the beach below the little blue penguins came out of the surf and proceeded to waddle up into the undergrowth for safety. Here there was a colony of nesting and recently hatched red-legged gulls too. Later we were delighted by the sighting of yellow-eyed penguins, thrilling.

The decision to travel to Stewart Island and from there to Ulva Island was so exciting as we found the most interesting endemics; the trees, ferns and plants that are all so special to those tiny islands included the miru, rimu and totara. Thankfully the rats have been eradicated leaving the island safe for the white-capped albatross, southern albatross, spotted, white and pied shags, friendly blue robins, brown treecreeper and kākā; as well as the large, brown flightless weka and the rifleman, which is as small as

Red-legged gulls

168

the eye of an albatross. Our guide, also called Ulva, was able to find them all for us. The umbrella ferns, marble tree and southern rata sickle ferns, cyathea and dicksonia (both can be traced directly back to the Gondwana supercontinent) also grew there healthily.

Yellow-eyed penguins

The numbers of tuataras, a prehistoric iguana-type lizard, are greatly endangered, but we did visit the art gallery/museum at Invercargill to 'encounter' Henry who hatched sometime in the late 19th century. To see the flightless, nocturnal kiwi we had to visit the park at the base of the Gondola in Queenstown. At Jackson Bay we finally sighted a tūī bird. A tiny young Fiordland crested penguin was obviously lost when we found it standing in the middle of our road towards Haast from the Tasman Sea calling for its mother. I quickly took an image before continuing in case I stressed it anymore. The poor thing, on such a hot day.

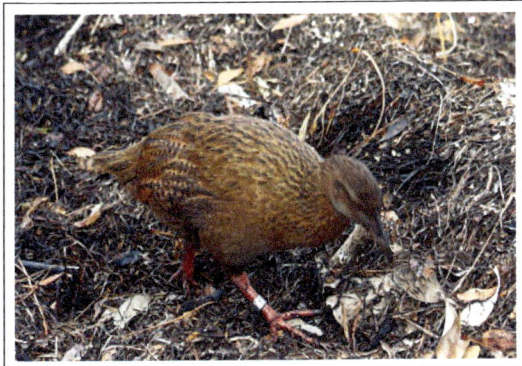

Weka

The birdlife at Havelock was worth investigating as were the green mussels for which it is famous! On the estuary we found godwit, banded dotterel, pied and variable oystercatcher, pied stilt, spoonbills, Caspian terns and black-backed gulls. Just outside Tauranga, near the Tuahu Track, we came to a forest of enormous coniferous kauri trees some 600 years old. Further onwards at Muriwai Heads, we found the tākapu Australasian gannet colony, a large seabird of the booby and gannet family, whose pungent odour guided us to see a wonderful sight and sound. The birds were so graceful in flight and in their swooping, flapping, feeding and nuzzling; complete with perfect markings including an antique gold-coloured head but sadly, just like the ugly duckling, the young are not at all beautiful!

Gannets

When sailing up the Kamchatka Peninsula the opportunity arose to fly to the Valley of Geysers inland from Petrapavlovsk. Here we were thrilled to encounter brown bears, who had come out of their den far earlier than the ones we discovered in the far distance further north.

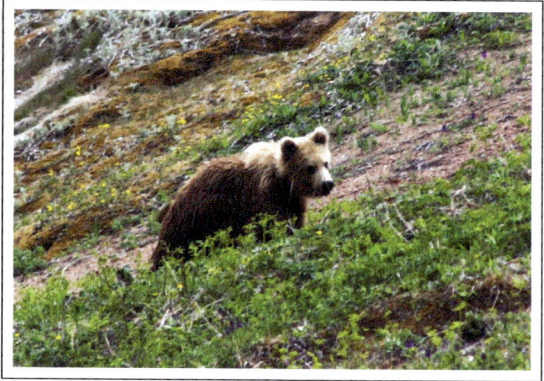

Brown bear

In South America, Ecuador is a country filled with endemic species. I was thrilled to see the pink freshwater dolphins, a potoo – oh so well disguised – as well as the largest

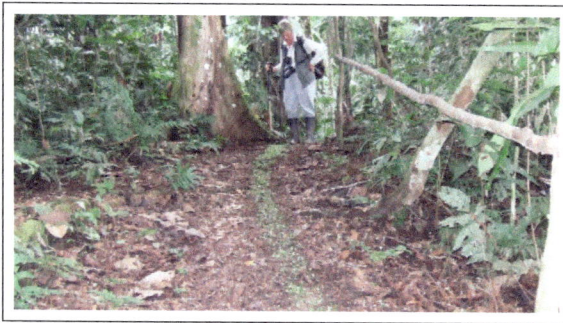

Leaf ants

butterflies ever, and frogs large and small. Deep in the Napo jungle we were just clambering up a steep slippery hill when we found leaf ants well and truly at work because their previous home appeared to have

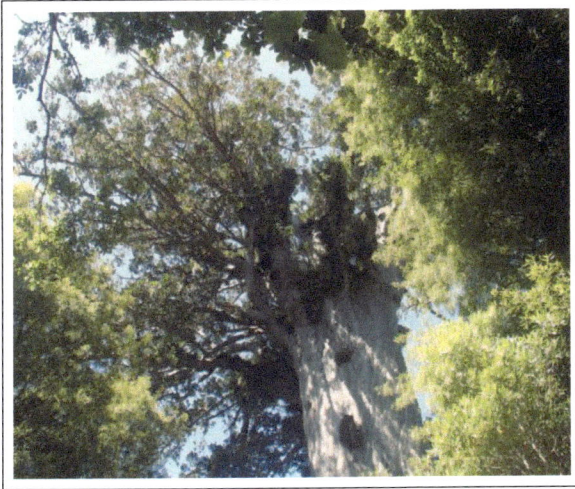

Tree Canopy

been flooded. In a rank 12 inches wide, they were working their way right up the hill to an enormously tall tree that they were climbing for young leaves and returning with their load to their new home, a truly astonishing sight. Parrots and parakeets in enormous flocks came to the various salt licks while the sound of howler monkeys resounded. It was the stinking turkeys that fascinated me the most while we were up on the Napo River.

This extraordinary bird is almost pre-historic, known as the 'hoatzin', and is a folivore who eats the leaves of trees and bushes found over water. It has an unusually large crop containing two chambers for the bacterial fermentation

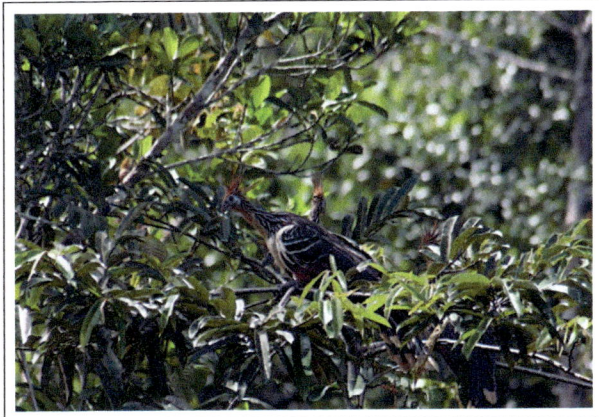

Hoatzin

of the unusual foliage. The indigenous tribes will only hunt these birds when in dire need. The chicks are unique as they have two claws on each wing which allow them, immediately on hatching, to scramble with their oversized feet around the branches without falling into the water beneath. If a predator finds them, they immediately drop into the water and swim under the surface to escape, using their clawed wings to climb back to the safety of the nest. How incredible it is that nature is always offering the biggest of surprises.

171

Many of the condors in the Ecuadorian mountains are being poisoned, as with the white-tailed vultures in Africa but we did visit an estancia where the condors are being helped, by being fed a couple of times a week and are now pleasingly increasing in numbers. At this same estancia we went off in the forlorn hope of sighting a spectacled bear, sadly we were not lucky!

The Cloud Forest of this diverse country offered us hard hiking with the most thrilling sightings of many different types of hummingbirds, but the greatest moment was when we finally found the cock-of-the-rock. We had to walk through the tropical rainforest to see this most territorial of birds with a lek that the magnificently plumed male guards with vigour; the females are not red but a dull brown with just a touch of the male's colour. The cock-of-the-rock is the iconic bird of the Mindo: the Cloud Forest of Ecuador.

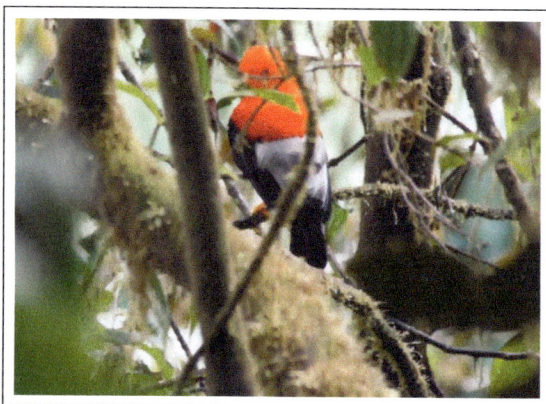

Cock-of-the-rock

On the Ecuadorian islands of Galapagos, I was overjoyed to see the red-breasted frigatebirds, sea lions, turtles, boobies, pelicans, marine iguana, starfish, stingray, the extraordinary Sally Lightfoot crabs, Chatham mockingbird, yellow warbler, ground and cactus finch, my favourite the tropicbird and of course the diverse tortoises including lonesome George who sadly has since died. Guatemala has even more endemics. I was thrilled after many determined treks up through the jungle on the side of an old volcano to find

Tortoise

a quetzal; the coati, agouti and social flycatcher amongst others were far easier to sight – no pain, no gain!

Still in South America, the jaw-dropping bird numbers in the Pantanal, Brazil is a sight that needs to be seen to be believed. Being driven along the Transpantaneira was most certainly 'a banquet' of sightings. Along the river we were of course working

Jaguar

Hyacinth macaws

hard to find the famed jaguar, which we achieved, along with giant otters, the yacare (a broad-snouted caiman) capybara, green iguana, rhea, capuchin monkeys, boat-billed herons and the jabiru stork. To be welcomed at Porto Jofre by nesting hyacinth

macaws and red ones too in several places was more than I could have wished. Here too I sighted about 30 nightjars sitting in the short grass, how amazing! As too, were the most enormous Amazonian water lilies out on the lake many both in bud and in full flower.

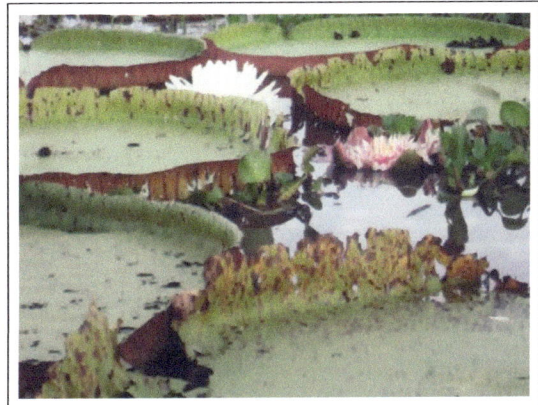

Amazonian water lilies

Travelling across the high altiplano of Bolivia and Peru it was a joy to see the locals with their domesticated llamas and alpacas; to sight both guanacos and vicuñas, the wild camelids, took longer but in the end we succeeded.

Chile being such a long country, has diverse flora and fauna from flamingos up in the Atacama Desert to penguins down in the south. Down there I was able to spot my first beaver too, incredible little workers redesigning the whole landscape by their labours. The many species of penguin are seen from here and the Galápagos southwards to the Pole.

Down on the Falkland Islands my breath was all but taken away by the joy of sitting amongst black-browed albatross, rockhopper and Magellanic penguins on West Point Island. The albatrosses were bonding, courting, mating, sitting on eggs, turning eggs, flying in, flying out, feeding upon the water, calling, pooing and even having the occasional scrap. It was mesmerising. Amongst all this activity the penguins hopped, waddled, called, bonded, courted, mated, sat on eggs, turned eggs, fed each other and squabbled occasionally but did not fly in! Down on the beach we found the endemic Falkland flightless steamer ducks, skuas, upland geese, Cobb's wren, black-throated finch, grass wren, tussock bird and Falkland thrush. Thank goodness for our bird guide, I would never have been able to identify all these glorious creatures. At Gypsy Cove and Yorke Bay I spotted night herons nesting beside turkey vultures, rock cormorants, two-banded plovers, white-rumped sandpipers, tyrants and thrushes along with dolphin and kelp gulls too.

Black-browed albatross

Night heron

We also visited a colony of gentoo penguins where we found the ever-predatory caracara, turkey buzzards and skuas, sharing the area with wrens, siskin and lark. The gorse, lichen, wrack, diddle-dee, berry-lobelia,

Pair of Kelp Geese

balsam bog, sea cabbage and sheep's sorrel grew hither and thither. It felt like heaven.

Across the waters towards South Georgia and the South Sandwich Islands the seabirds were prevalent; also numerous were different albatrosses, petrels, skuas, shags, sheathbills, gulls, shearwaters, prions and terns. Towards Elephant Island we began to see seals, snow petrels, king penguins and kelp gulls. Finally, arriving at King Haakon Bay, where the southern shore was rat free, it was well populated by burrowing petrels, blue petrels, Antarctic prions and seals as well as the great elephant seals. The endemic flora and fauna suffered immeasurably with the whaling that came to South Georgia when the ships brought rats that soon multiplied. Most of the animals introduced were to be used as food: rabbits, sheep, pigs, goats, horses, cattle, chickens and ducks. Thankfully

King penguins

none of these deliberate introductions could establish populations in that environment but between 1911 and 1925, 22 reindeer were brought to the island from Norway and by 2012 they numbered around 3,000. The native flora did not evolve in the presence of such

175

Elephant seal

herbivores and therefore suffered enormously from their grazing. Since then, there has been a terrific campaign to rid the island of the rats and to cull all the reindeer. Meanwhile we ate venison which happened to be one of the last to be culled. I was thrilled to see both the South Georgia pipit and pintail, now apparently breeding well. At Gold Harbour I was overjoyed to spot an Antarctic fur seal with twins amongst all the other wildlife living that amazing life at the 'end of the world'.

Travelling much further north to finally spot a narwhal was a long-held wish satisfied. I have always had a fond fascination for these toothed whales with their extraordinary helical tusk, and for the white beluga whale, both whales were seen up in the Arctic waters of the Northwest Passage. In Isabela Bay we were so

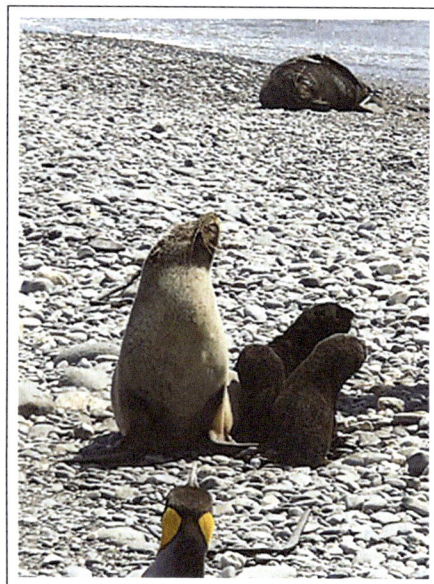
Fur seal with twins

lucky to see 10% of the world's population of bowhead whales. This bay is now a nature reserve as it is where they gather to clean themselves given the shallow waters with a high concentration of fresh water; while I watched them in awe some king eider came flying by, while little auks and more kittiwakes were twirling around the ship. Still up in the Northwest Province, when we sailed near land, I was able to sight musk oxen, arctic fox, red-throated divers, snow geese, many other seabirds and of course polar bears.

Walrus

Orca

Orca

'The Arctic has a strange stillness that no other wilderness knows' is written on the front of my trip's diary. The blood began to rush when out at sea we experienced a wonderful pod of orca whales who proceeded to swim beneath the boat, the first sighting to be recorded that year. We had just visited the Franklin expedition graves when we not only met up with

Polar bears

our sister ship the *Vavalov* who was on her way to search successfully for the *Erebus*, but also, we came across polar bears. The joy.

Having 'zodiaced' through rough waters from our boat to a steep pebble beach and onto staggeringly beautiful tundra at Sorgfjorden, off Svalbard,

Walrus

we found a walrus 'haul out'. There were lots of them lying about on the beach while three were having the time of their life in the water. I don't know why but I have always been keen to see these enormous creatures and like the narwhal, it was a wish satisfied. The walrus are relatively long-living, social animals who have played a prominent role in the lives of the indigenous Arctic people, who have used their meat, fat, tusks, skin and bone.

Here in Svalbard, I was entranced by the wildflowers, each delicate, diverse and so close to the ground. The forest was just four inches high, the colours so subtle and their season extremely short, light and twilight triggering both growth and closure. Research shows that these Arctic-alpine plants are also affected by touch whether by finger or by sand and pebbles, either way it will bring on lockdown. The autumn storms will bring total closure so that the plants retain their nutrients. The incredible migration of Arctic terns from their breeding grounds here on Svalbard down to their

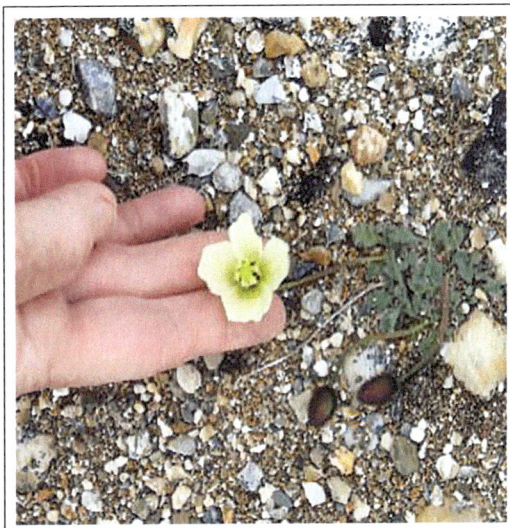

Svalbard poppy

winter-feeding grounds of the Antarctic is well known, but I was so thrilled to find a colony nesting down on the estuary, not shy to bombard me if I came too close for their comfort. We were in Longyearbyen, the capital of Svalbard, for only a couple of hours and I found both eider ducks and barnacle geese with their young alongside the husky kennels!

Further south in Norway's northern district I was overjoyed to travel with the Sámi and their reindeer herd travelling from their winter pastures to the summer grounds at Nordkapp. The Sámi family's main member of staff was Nestor, who was their reindeer dog, what a fantastic animal. Not unlike a sheepdog and similarly able. We failed to sight a wolverine which was just as well as they are the number one predator to the

Reindeer dog

Migrating reindeer

reindeer but once we had handed in our skidoos and were waiting for our Hurtigruten boat we rested up in a hotel where I found that beautiful creature up on the bar – stuffed of course!

Much nearer to home the furthest island of the Outer Hebrides, St Kilda along with the mighty rock faces of Scarp, Boreray, Stac Lee and Stac an Armin are home to enormous colonies of shags, gannets, puffins, razorbills, kittiwakes, fulmars, eider ducks and oystercatchers. There are St Kilda skuas, snipe, the St Kilda wren and rock pipits too. Along with Soay and Hirta they form what is known as the 'St Kilda archipelago', the remains of an extinct volcano which rose from the seas 50-60 million years ago.

As I climbed beside the Soay sheep above Village Bay, St Kilda, I spotted numerous painted lady butterflies feeding on the sea thrift. It is truly amazing how these fragile creatures fly from North Africa and Southern

St Kilda sheep

Europe to reach this small group of islands. Near the top of the hill at Ruabhal I encountered the bonxies (the great skuas) who certainly did not tolerate invaders into their territory and would swoop down trying to land a beak or talon on human flesh! Machair, a Gaelic word meaning 'fertile' refers to a unique habitat found only on the exposed west-facing shores

Skuas – bonxies

of Scotland and Ireland. It is an ideal nesting place for the fulmars who, given an intruder, defensively project vomit, an unpleasant smelling oleaginous fluid, at its aggressor!

Landing on Taransay there was more machair growing. Here we found

Arctic tern

otter tracks and many flowers including orchids, heartsease, marsh-marigolds, sundews, bog asphodel and ragged-robin. The golden plovers were nesting, alongside terns and oystercatchers while the eider duck was taking her ducklings off for their first swim. Back on Skye, I watched five sea eagles (white-tailed eagles) who have

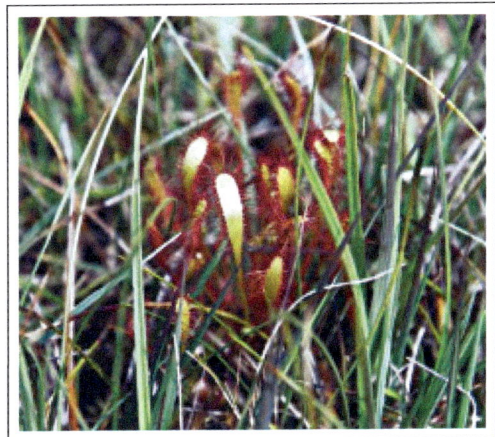

Sundews

181

a wingspan of up to eight feet (2.5m) up on the hillside above Uig. These are increasing further across the Highlands, we recently saw them flying above the Insh Marshes near Kingussie in the Cairngorms National Park. This morning before I returned home to write this chapter in South Warwickshire, I watched a red kite being mobbed by a crow, and across the plough the larks were singing and performing their mating flight dance. Some species are declining rapidly but others most interestingly extend their strongholds which is why I find searching, however difficult and uncomfortable, so satisfying.

Thankfully I started my love of nature at a very young age and maybe because I was given a china elephant for an early birthday present, they have been my favourite creature. Never am I happier than when I am in the company of either the Indian or African species.

Elephants on the Chobe

As long as I can, I will continue to discover with enthusiasm remembering that no pain, no gain is my motto!

Chapter 16
Finally Travels Resume After the Pandemic

After so much time having so many trips cut and pasted because of the ongoing pandemic finally there came the green light to fly off to visit my friend and travelling partner in Florida before flying to Baja, the Bay of Mexico. This trip had been on my wish list for many years, having asked Santiago from Think Galápagos to organise an expedition there.

I was surprised how nervous I was with the thought of all the online airport requirements that are now in place. Not used to mobile phones and modern technology, feeling as I did, one would have thought that I had never travelled before! But once at Heathrow Airport it was a doddle – why had I been in such a state? Suffice it to say, I am back on track.

Our expedition was a triumph especially when the grey whales that we had particularly travelled to witness came to us in great numbers. These gentle giants, the size of two buses came up to the side of our tiny fishing boats and allowed us to pat them, splash them and of course gain the most incredible photographs. These females come down to the Bay of Mexico all the way from the Bering Sea where, as baleen feeders they feed on krill etc., to give birth or mate.

There is no food for these gentle giants in these waters, but they are safe from predators, namely orcas, but the mothers have to provide about 50lbs of milk for their calf each day. The calf must grow and learn extremely quickly.

Once strong enough they take the long journey back up to the Bering Sea to enjoy the lush food awaiting them. On their way they must avoid the orcas and the shipping traffic but sadly, suffer from the interruptions of the engine sounds that cause so many problems to our underwater creatures.

The males also come south for the chance to mate with those females who are 'in season'. This we encountered, being totally staggered at the sight of 'Pink Floyd' who came up above the surface before sinking fast back down into the waters. So surprised were we that no one took a photo, but I believe we all had tears in our eyes with astonishment at its magnitude!

Apparently over the last 20 or so years the mothers have been teaching their calves to go up to the boats to communicate; the fishermen had noticed this and realised that the tourist business was there for them to offer during this short period. They also noticed that if they had youngsters in their boat the likelihood of the grey whale coming beside was greater. I too, noticed

this when a boat with three parents and their many children was soon the young whale's preference to the other boat filled with adults with mega cameras and a drone.

Of course, all trips have their crises, which one has to take as par for the course – or ride! Our van produced the sound of a traction engine, which was very quickly replaced; the sole of my foot was badly cut by razor-sharp shells when wading to shore, having been separated from my water shoes, and our boat conked out just at the end of a whale watching safari,

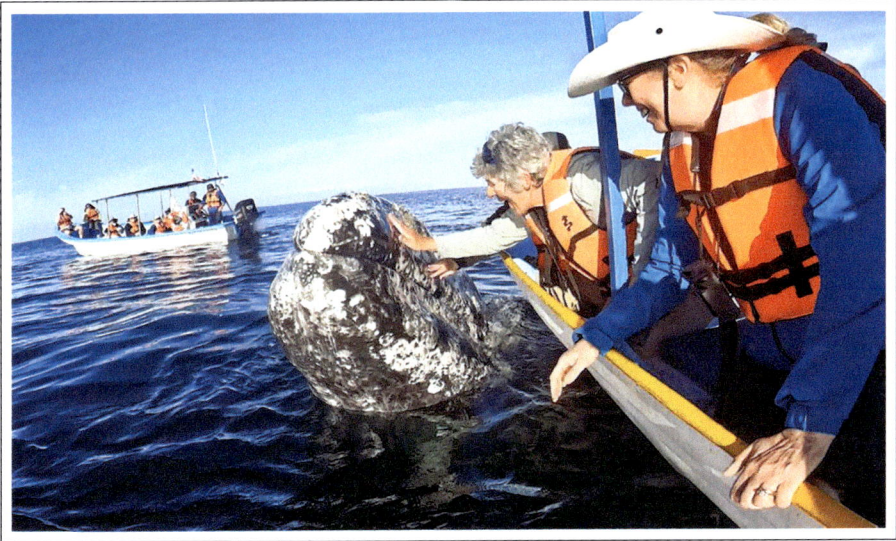

which caused us to have to transfer to another tiny boat mid water – a challenge and inevitably a good laugh, since no one dropped into the 'drink'!

Along with the astonishment at our good luck, our experiences have been nothing but sheer joy. On reflection of that incredible experience I could not but think that these mothers, these great gentle giants of the ocean, were teaching us a very big lesson if we would but listen.

I truly believe they were saying to us "YOU HAVE STOPPED WHALING, THANK YOU – NOW AND ONLY NOW, DO WE TRUST YOU WITH OUR BABIES – ENJOY".

What a wonderful world we live in, to enjoy, to learn and not to spoil. Remember:

"It is not the number of breaths you breathe in your lifetime; it is the amount of times your breath is taken away".

Thankfully, I am back on track!

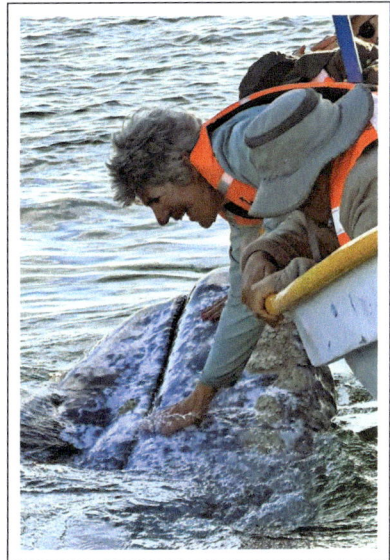